The
Sandcastles Guide
to
Starting and
Managing Your
Own Wedding-Planning
Business

The
Sandcastles Guide
to
Starting and
Managing Your
Own Wedding-Planning
Business

✦

How to Enjoy a Career in One of Today's Most Exciting Professions

Shari Beck

iUniverse, Inc.
New York Lincoln Shanghai

The Sandcastles Guide to Starting and Managing Your Own Wedding-Planning Business
How to Enjoy a Career in One of Today's Most Exciting Professions

iUniverse books may be ordered through booksellers or by contacting:

iUniverse
2021 Pine Lake Road, Suite 100
Lincoln, NE 68512
www.iuniverse.com
1-800-Authors (1-800-288-4677)

ISBN: 978-0-595-43762-7 (pbk)
ISBN: 978-0-595-88090-4 (ebk)

Printed in the United States of America

This book is dedicated to my husband, Fred Beck, who pretended to listen when I rambled on about weddings, and who cooked my dinner as I sat night after night at the computer;

To my daughter, Laura, whose wedding was the best I ever planned;

And to the many aspiring wedding planners I have met over the years, who were the reason I decided to write it in the first place.

Contents

INTRODUCTION

The Sandcastles Guide to Starting and Managing Your Own Wedding-Planning Business is not a book about planning a wedding. You will not read about the proper etiquette for a receiving line, planning altar flowers for the ceremony, or the correct wording of a wedding invitation. If you are reading this book, you are either planning to open your own business, or you have already done so and wish to learn how to keep it running smoothly and profitably.

The information in this book has come from my own experience and from business administration courses I have taken. Anything involving business administration has been adapted for wedding planning—benefit selling for example. The bride-to-be will expect different benefits from planning her wedding than she will from buying a new car.

This book will not solve your day-to-day problems. You will still have days when nothing seems to go right. Hopefully, this book will play an important role in making sure those days are few and far between.

This book is not intended to be legal or financial advice. I am neither a lawyer nor an accountant. Nothing can replace a good working relationship with both.

This book will not bring you more clients, nor will it make your business successful. Only *you* can do that. You breathe life into your business, nurture it, and watch it grow. In these pages you will find information, advice, and ideas, but you alone can apply them and make them work for you.

1

STARTING YOUR BUSINESS

Find Your Future in Your Past

Every wedding planner has her own personal story. No doubt you do, too—a story of how you came to be interested in a career in this business. You may have helped so many friends plan their weddings that you have decided to do it for a living. Maybe you have always had a flair for organizing details and events. Perhaps you have been in the field of hospitality and are accustomed to planning events and working with caterers.

Those who know me through *Sandcastles* are familiar with my story. My background is in the field of interior design; before opening *Sandcastles*, I ran *Interior Motives* for twelve years. Wedding planning was something I had never considered, until that fateful day …

I had been hired by a couple who were designing their dream home. They were to move into it immediately upon returning from their honeymoon. My job was to oversee the work in their absence. Our small talk turned to the plans they were making for their upcoming wedding. Since my work as a decorator involved such things as colors, fabrics, and flower arrangements, they asked my advice. Some time later, they referred me to another couple they knew—not to design their home, but to help them plan their wedding! I enjoyed it so much that I added "Wedding Design" to my list of services. Eventually, I had to make the decision to quit decorating in favor of wedding planning. It was a move I have never regretted.

Like interior design, many careers can lead to planning weddings, including fashion design and merchandising, catering, floral design, dressmaking, and photography. Or, you may have a background in business and wish to combine it with your creative side.

In any case, your past has led you to where you are right now. Whether you are just starting your wedding-planning business, or are refreshing your knowledge after several years, you can look forward to years of enjoyment in one of today's fastest-growing professions!

Your formal education has prepared you for your new career in ways that you may have never considered. You have an advantage if you have taken courses in

- merchandising
- fashion
- marketing
- advertising
- business administration
- hospitality
- fine arts
- interior design
- travel and tourism

You have wedding-planning experience if you have ever

- planned your own wedding
- helped a friend or relative plan their wedding
- been a bridesmaid or maid of honor

Knowledge of weddings and etiquette alone will suffice if you will be working for someone else. Since you are interested in running your own business, however, you must also develop the knowledge and skills involved in managing day-to-day operations. Take night school classes and read everything you can.

Finding Your Niche

Weddings are such big business that it is impossible to cover the entire market. That's why it is important that you identify and occupy your share of the industry.

A **"Wedding Day Director"** or **"Wedding Day Coordinator"** will step in after the bride and groom have made their plans. As a general rule, this job involves the rehearsal, the wedding day, and the reception. Some wedding coordinators are recommended by their church and handle only the rehearsal and ceremony. This is the easiest job to price by the hour.

A **"Bridal Consultant"** usually works for a particular store, and is an expert in her field. There are bridal consultants who deal with wedding fashions, invitations, and the gift registry.

A **"Wedding Planner"** or a **"Wedding Consultant"** may do as little as a one-hour consultation or she may plan the entire wedding. She meets with the couple, assists them in contracting vendors, is on hand the day of the wedding (and long into the night), and takes care of the countless little things that need attention. People envy her because her job is "glamorous" and "romantic." (Right now it's 11:10 on a Friday night, and here I am sitting at the computer; how's *that* for glamorous?)

Must You Be Certified?

At this time, there is no government regulation of the wedding-planning industry. It is perfectly legal to open a wedding-planning business with no formal education or training. However, those who do so are at a disadvantage in two very important aspects:

- They have to learn for themselves when it comes to the logistics and techniques of wedding planning.

- Their clients may doubt their knowledge and expertise.

This is not necessarily well-founded. Many uncertified wedding planners are very well-informed and extremely talented. However, if I were a bride about to hire an uncertified wedding planner, I would wonder if I could do just as well myself.

There is no doubt about it—a certificate hanging on your office wall could very well mean the difference between signing a contract for a wedding and losing the job.

There are many certification courses on the market. I took two different ones, but I found that they were lacking on the business end. I supplemented my training with college courses in business administration. This made my education quite expensive, but it ultimately lead me to my next venture—I combined all of my courses into the *Sandcastles Wedding Consultant Certification Programme.* Our graduates are well-trained and have the confidence to plan any wedding. We have students from all over the world, thanks to our home-study format and affordable payment plan. If you are interested in becoming certified and would like to find out more about our course, visit our Web site, *www.sandcastles.sharibeck.com.*

The Attributes of the Wedding Planner

Analytical Thinker: This is a business in which you must be able to look at problems, analyze them, and solve them—sometimes on the spot. You must deal with spaces, people, time, and tangibles. You are an expert in time and motion management. It is necessary to work with both sides of the brain—the right side for creativity and the left side for organization.

Creative: You decorate reception halls and color-coordinate flowers to bridesmaids' dresses. You deal in color, fabrics, and lighting. In other words, you literally "design" the wedding.

Social: You must be friendly, outgoing, and genuine. You have to be honest, candid, and direct, yet at the same time tactful. A "people person" makes the best wedding planner!

Entrepreneurial: You are a professional business woman as well as a creative wedding designer. You have a side that the bride rarely sees—the organized administrator.

Professional: Throughout the entire wedding-planning process, you must remain calm and confident. You must be able to work against deadlines and be ready to answer all questions, no matter how insignificant they may seem.

Assured: You must keep up-to-date on all aspects of the wedding industry and be sure of your abilities to provide the public with a valuable service. You are able to do the impossible immediately!

Keeping Your Present Job

Many wedding planners like to start their businesses while they still have the safety net of a steady job. Others have no intention of quitting their present jobs; they are happy to plan weddings "on the side." Everyone in this position falls into one of two categories: those who are doing what they do with the knowledge and blessing of their employer, and those who are running a part-time business against company rules.

To tell or not to tell? Be sure before you make the decision. Check the employee handbook; usually, it will spell out the company's policy on this issue. Most companies don't have a problem as long as there is no conflict of interest. Some employees go so far as to set themselves up as consultants within their area of expertise. In other words, they are not only working for the competition, they *are* the competition. Although this may not be the case in your situation, many employers feel that it is not in the best interest of the company to have employees with outside business interests.

At the other end of the spectrum is the boss who doesn't mind you having a part-time business, and who may even send you a few clients. You will have to prove yourself by never letting your work take a backseat to your business. You must be willing to work as hard as you ever did, and with as much enthusiasm as always. Do not refuse to put in overtime if requested. Never drag yourself in on Monday morning after a weekend wedding. Be careful never to conduct yourself in any way that will cheapen your image or that of the company for which you work. And, never take time off to show clients a reception venue or to meet with your florist.

If you have decided to let your employer in on your secret, explain your position. You have another interest which in no way conflicts with the company's business. Furthermore, it does not interfere with the superb job you have been doing and will continue to do. You are not asking permission to plan weddings. You are merely filling him in so he won't be in the dark if he sees your advertising, or when he calls you at home and your voice mail is obviously that of a home business.

You may decide to keep your business small, and work at your present job indefinitely; many wedding planners do. When the time comes to devote yourself to your business on a full-time basis, you'll know. If this time comes, don't abruptly quit. Let your employer know several months in advance, and offer to train your successor. Never burn your bridges. You never know who knows someone who is getting married!

Never, *ever* use the company telephone, or company time, to call your vendors or clients. The same rule applies to the office computer. Use your cell phone to check your messages on your coffee break or lunch hour. Anything that can't wait until you get home can be taken care of at these times. You may wish to call from your car or a nearby restaurant.

Do not tell *anyone* about your business until you have told your employer. This includes the girl in the next office who is getting married! You owe him this courtesy, and we all know how gossip tends to spread.

Never take time off to meet with clients during the day. Remember an important marketing strategy: take a perceived negative and turn it into a positive. De-emphasize that fact that you are unavailable during the day; emphasize the fact that you are available evenings and weekends, so that your clients never have to take time off work to meet with you. Consider breakfast meetings with clients and business contacts.

Don't be afraid to tell clients that yours is a part-time business. I know several professionals who work only three days a week. If by some chance you should lose the client, don't worry. There will be plenty of others.

Never be tempted to take office supplies for your own use. It's still stealing, even if "everybody does it."

Demographics and Market Analysis

The demographics of a particular area will give you such information as population, age, and income level. It is important that you study the results of demographic surveys for the area in which you intend to set up your business. Contact your local municipal office for information on how to obtain these.

When you have the survey results, organize the information so that you can examine it. You will need the statistics in each category for the town or city in which you are interested, as well as figures for a five-mile radius, a twenty-five-mile radius, and a hundred-mile radius.

Population: Determine the total population, as well as the breakdown for each of the geographic ranges.

Income: For each of the geographic ranges, find the number of households with an income of

- under $40,000
- $40,000-$60,000
- $60,000-$80,000
- over $80,000

Age: Determine the number of people in each age bracket

- 15-20
- 21-30
- 31-40
- 41-60
- over 60

You will then analyze your potential market. Gone are the days when you could rely only on young brides. Second weddings are becoming just as elaborate as first weddings, and need your services just as badly. As well, career women are marrying later and paying more for their weddings (they are also too busy to do their own planning). If this is the demographic picture you get of the area, go ahead and set up your office there. However, if you find that you are in an area of young families with children under the age of two, or a large percentage of retirees, you may wish to locate elsewhere. Likewise, a wedding-planning business will not do well in areas where there is widespread unemployment and little disposable income.

Most likely you are thinking of starting a home business, and the area you study will be that in which you live. However, it may occur to you that it would be more feasible to obtain space in a small office and commute to your business. Do the math: compare the buying power of your area, the obvious savings of working from home, and the costs of renting in a more affluent area. You may decide to open your home office but target your advertising at another area.

You must determine your "market share." In order to know what the market will bear, research other wedding-related businesses in your area. Some people find it embarrassing to call other businesses and ask them pointed questions, so they pretend to be an interested bride. Don't pose as a potential client; it's dishonest and tacky. Call and introduce yourself. Tell them why you called. There is a slight chance that they won't speak with you—some people are insecure and intimidated by competition. Hang up and call someone who is more confident. Make a new friend and colleague.

Ask how many weddings they plan in a year, the average age of their brides, and the average cost of their weddings. When you explore other wedding businesses you will develop a picture of the industry in your area. You will find out which aspects are saturated and which are lacking. Find a need and fill it—claim your own little corner of the market.

Your Business Image

The very fact that you are a wedding planner will give you an image in people's minds—romance, elegance and glamour. Although the job is sometimes very *un*romantic, we can let them think what they want, right?

Choose a specific image for your business. Will you plan weddings on limited budgets, or will you cater to the carriage trade, doing mostly society weddings? Will you specialize in dramatic weddings with special effects, or will your weddings be ultra-traditional? Whatever your style, it will create an image for your business.

Your choice of business name will reflect this image. So will the style of your business cards and brochures. Your office will be decorated accordingly, and it will even show in how you dress for meetings.

Choose a business image that is close to your own personality. This is not something you can fake; you are cheating yourself and your clients if you are trying to be something you're not. You will plan all kinds of weddings for all kinds of clients. Regardless, you will leave your signature on all your weddings.

Use a "tag line" to convey a benefit and cause an emotional reaction. Jot down some of the benefits and emotions you wish to invoke, and come up with the tag line which best suits your particular business. If you are looking for ideas, try some of these:

- The wedding of your dreams is now a reality

- A wedding as beautiful as your love

- A wedding as elegant as you are

- Your wedding, your way

- You tie the knot, we'll take care of the loose ends

- Down the aisle with style

Business Name and Logo

Naming a business is like naming a baby. The name will stay with the business all its life and must fit its personality. Luckily, the business has a controllable and predictable future. That makes the naming process easier.

You might choose a name related to weddings. Or, you may wish to use your own name, such as "Weddings by Susan," or "Barbara Jones and Associates." The second has no connection to weddings, and can be used if you do other consulting as well.

After you have several ideas in mind, begin to narrow down your choices. First, be sure that no one is already using the name. Look in the Yellow Pages, and conduct an Internet search on the name. Do keep in mind, though, that you must do a formal name search when you register the business.

Perhaps you will design a logo. Although a logo is not absolutely necessary, it is a visual representation that gives your business instant recognition. If you are artistic, draw the logo and have it reproduced in several sizes to suit various purposes, as such business cards, letterhead, advertising, etc. If you would rather not do the artwork yourself, a graphic designer can do it for you. A less costly alternative may be to have the logo drawn when you order your business cards.

Registering Your Business

You will not be able to use your business name until you register it with your local government agency. In some areas, if you are planning to do business as a sole proprietor under your own name, you do not need to register. This does not mean having your name as part of the business name, as in "Weddings by Mary Jones," but simply the name "Mary Jones."

Your first step is to conduct a formal name search. Have several names in mind, in case someone is already using your first choice. Each variation counts as a separate search, but the fees are nominal and it's well worth the cost. Using someone else's name could involve you in a lawsuit; at the very least, you could be ordered to stop doing business under that name, and your advertising dollars would be wasted.

The name search and registration can be done at the same time. In some areas land-registry offices and government information centers have self-serve workstations which you can use to complete the entire process. The fee can be paid with your credit card and the registration mailed to you. It is also possible to register a business over the Internet.

If you will be hiring employees, determine the legal requirements for your area and obtain the correct forms.

Business Structure

There are three types of business structure: sole proprietorship, partnership, and corporation. Ninety-nine percent of wedding planners who operate their businesses from home are sole proprietors.

A **sole proprietor** is a self-employed person who is the only owner of a business. This is the simplest and least expensive type of business ownership, as it can be formed without a lawyer. Forming a sole proprietorship is as simple as registering a business name, opening a bank account, and taking out your first ad in your local newspaper.

As with everything else in business, there are advantages and disadvantages. The advantages are many: you are your own boss, you answer to no one, and all profits belong solely to you. The main disadvantage is that you and your business are one and the same. A lawsuit against the business is a lawsuit against you. You are personally liable for business debts. When you die, your business dies with you.

A **partnership** exists when two or more people go into business together. Each partner will be responsible for a percentage of the financial outlay, and will be entitled to the same percentage of the profits. Most partners are "general partners," but it is possible to have a "limited partner" if an individual wishes to invest in the business without taking part in the day-to-day operations.

A significant advantage is that you do not have to fund your new venture alone. As well, each partner will bring her own unique strengths and talents to the business, and is personally responsible for her portion of the debts. Be aware, though, that if your partner cannot pay her share, or if she walks out on the business, you will have to come up with the money. If you have not chosen your partners well, you could end up in a situation messier than a divorce.

A partnership agreement must be drawn up by a lawyer. It will cover such things as each partner's expected contributions and responsibilities, dissolution of the partnership, and the ratio of ownership. To prepare for the possibility that one of you could die, your lawyer can arrange a type of life insurance that will enable the surviving partner to buy out the family of the deceased partner. Otherwise, you can arrange to have the business terminate upon the death of one of the partners.

In a **corporation,** you and your business are two separate legal entities. It is the most complex and expensive type of business to form. In a corporation, owners hold shares of the company's stock. If you are the only member of your company, you own all the stock.

The main advantage of incorporation is that you are not personally responsible for the debts of the business. As well, a small business that is incorporated has more credibility, making it easier to get a bank loan. The biggest disadvantage is the amount of complex paperwork involved. There are reports to fill out, a very complicated taxation process, and higher income taxes. You will be taxed twice: corporate tax on the corporation and personal tax on the income you draw from the business.

If you decide to end your business, the corporation can be sold, transferred, bankrupted, or dissolved. The business does not die when you do, and can be willed to your heirs.

You must decide which structure to use before registering your business or its name. Only a corporation can use "Ltd," "Limited," or "Inc." A corporation may also register a "style name." For example, if your corporate name is "Mary Jones

Enterprises, Limited," but you want the public to identify you with the wedding industry, you could register "Weddings by Mary" as your style name.

Developing Your Business Plan

A business plan is necessary for getting a bank loan, but it is so much more. It is the most effective way to pinpoint internal and external forces that will affect your business, and it forces you to come up with possible solutions. It also gives you an opportunity to assess your business and personal goals, and allows you to chart your progress. Even if you are able to open your business without borrowing money, you still need a business plan. Read ahead to the pages on budgets, setting your fees, and office equipment, as you will be using this information when developing your business plan.

The business plan must be typed, double-spaced. If you take the time to have it professionally bound, it will make your presentation all the more impressive. The components of a formal business plan are as follows:

TITLE PAGE:

Include the business name, your name, the date, and the time period covered by the business plan.

TABLE OF CONTENTS:

Neatly number all pages, which you will reference in the table of contents.

SUMMARY OF THE BUSINESS:

Provide a short outline of the business in two or three pages. Many lenders use this summary to decide if they want to read any farther, so this is your opportunity to gain their interest. Highlight the most important features of your business.

BACKGROUND OF THE BUSINESS:

Provide an outline of the business to the lender. Include the owners of the business (yourself and any partners you may have), planned start-up date, any previous financing, a description of the industry (including trends and markets), your current market area, and target clients.

GOALS AND OBJECTIVES:

State these in dollars and volume. Talk about your long-term goals, such as expansion or incorporation. Forecast where you want your business to be next year, three years from now, and five years from now.

OPERATIONS:

Outline your business operations. Although the many aspects of planning a wedding are obvious to you, they are not obvious to your bank manager. Give the costs of running your business from your home, and explain why this is a good option for you. Talk about your mortgage and taxes, as well as any renovations that your business has made necessary. Describe any special purchases you plan to make in the future.

KEY PERSONNEL:

You are the heart of your business—sell yourself! Include an up-to-date resume and tell how your past education and experience has led you to this point. Describe the back-up plan you have in case of illness. If you have other people on your team, show where they enter the picture. Look for any gaps in your abilities that can affect your business, and show how you plan to overcome them.

MARKETING PLAN:

Show that you are aware of the general economy, and that you have knowledge of your competition. If you offer a service that no other wedding planner does, give the details. Talk about the size of the market and your proposed share of that market. Speak in terms of lifestyle, implications of change, and disposable income. Give the strategic details of where you are, where you want to go, and how you plan to get there. Your marketing concept should be based on service, price, and promotion. If you have a brochure or any other printed material, include it here.

FINANCIAL PLAN:

Explain your month-by-month projected income and expenses. Determine your profit or loss. The lender needs to be certain that you are capable of repaying the loan; it will be evident from the information you have provided here. As an added bonus, you will be able to read the projected budget backwards: if you need to make $_ you must provide $_ worth of services. Include a separate sheet on start-up costs.

SUPPLIERS:

List companies with whom you have done business in the past, or plan to in the future.

Funding Your New Business Venture

Unless you have a large nest-egg saved for the purpose, you will have to raise the money to start your wedding-planning business. It is impossible to give you a dollar figure, as each case is unique. To arrive at your own figures, see Chapter 4 for a list of equipment that you will need. Add to that:

- business registration

- office supplies

- insurance

- utilities

- advertising

- business cards

- letterhead

- legal fees

- consulting fees

- extra for emergencies

If you have the savings to go ahead, consider yourself lucky. Most new wedding planners need to borrow the money, either from individuals or by means of a bank loan. Family and friends are not the best sources of funding for business ventures. Families have been torn apart over money issues, and friendships are equally vulnerable. If you do decide to borrow, have papers drawn up to specify the principal amount, interest rate, monthly payments, and due dates. Don't take advantage of the situation by falling behind on your payments.

If you will be borrowing from the bank, take your business plan with you to the meeting. Don't be intimidated by the thought of sitting down with your bank manager—you are now a business woman!

The Business Bank Account

You would be surprised how many wedding planners operate their businesses from their own personal bank accounts. Others open a separate account in their own name for business use alone, which is not much better. Every professional business woman must apply for a business checking account (chequing in Canada). Usually, all it takes is proof of business registration and a credit check on you.

The service charges for a business account are higher than those for a personal account, but can be written off as a business expense. Most importantly, the business account will allow you to keep your personal money separate from the business money, saving you and your accountant many headaches.

The bank will also provide you with a banking machine card with the business name printed on it. Check with your individual bank regarding service charges; as a rule, if you use the card at another bank, extra fees apply.

The bank account must be reconciled monthly. The process can be broken down into four simple steps:

- Enter the closing balance shown on the statement.

- Compare your bank statement with your record of checks and deposits.

- Add any unlisted deposits to the closing balance; deduct any outstanding checks.

- Deduct any service charges shown on the statement.

Insurance

Speak to your insurance broker about your existing homeowner's insurance. Determine what is and is not included in that policy. You have invested (or will soon be investing) in an office full of valuable equipment, and you need to be covered in case of fire or theft. If you will be applying for a bank loan, insurance is mandatory.

Liability insurance is also worth looking into. A wedding planner contracts work to other businesses, which are liable for their own acts, errors, or omissions. Therefore, if the entire wedding party comes down with food poisoning, the caterer is legally responsible, not you. However, if a client should be injured while meeting with you at your home office, you will be liable.

Tax Permits

Every wedding planner should apply for a retail sales tax permit. If you plan to sell products, such as centerpieces or ring pillows, it is required by law.

If you are purchasing regularly from a particular source, file a "Purchase Exemption Certificate." You will then collect the tax when you sell the items and periodically remit this tax to the government. Sales tax is charged only within your geographical area.

In Canada, Goods and Services Tax (GST) is charged in addition to the applicable sales tax on merchandise, regardless of where you live. As the name implies, GST is also charged on services, including wedding-planning services, if your business makes over $30,000 in a year. The "Government" section of your local telephone book will guide you to the appropriate office.

Many business owners prefer to quote a price that includes all taxes. This is especially true in a profession such as ours. There is nothing more *unromantic* than paying tax on your wedding-planning fees! Consult your accountant if you have any questions.

Business Cards and Letterhead

Business cards are often the client's first impression of you and your business. Your card should say a great deal about both. It should be high-quality, easy to read, and reflective of your business image.

Your printer has a selection of card stock from which you may choose. There are many different surfaces, but the most popular are glossy stock and linen stock. Glossy business cards are usually more colorful, often with no white area at all. Linen stock cards are printed in one or two colors, possibly three. They are often printed using thermography, giving the ink a raised appearance.

Prices vary, depending on such factors as the addition of a second (or third) color. It is always worthwhile to order in larger quantities. The cost is only slightly higher for twice as many cards. Before ordering your cards, do a sketch of the finished appearance. This will show the printer how you want the card to be laid out. Include the business name, your name, telephone number, logo, e-mail, and Web site. You might choose not to include your address.

Have your letterhead and envelopes printed at the same time as your business cards. Ideally, the paper color should match the card stock; the ink color should also be the same. If you plan to have your logo on your letterhead and business cards, supply a clear copy to the printer.

A final word of advice: always return to the printer to proofread cards and letterhead before they are printed. If this is very inconvenient, they may be willing to fax you the proof and wait for your final approval by telephone, but not all printers will do this.

Brochures

Your brochure is the bride's first opportunity to familiarize herself with your business. Describe the services you offer, and project your personality and business image. As with business cards, prices vary. The more you order, the more cost-effective it becomes.

Brochures are usually triple-folded. The front will display your business name and logo; the text will be inside. Software is available to help you design brochures using your computer. Be sure to use high-quality paper, and at all costs avoid giving your brochure a homemade appearance.

An alternative to the triple-folded brochure is the portfolio format. It's more expensive, but it's worth it, as it gives a more upscale appearance. All business supply stores sell card-stock portfolio covers. Each side has a pocket to hold your literature and a place to insert your business card. All that's left for you to do is decide what to include. You can change the contents of the brochure simply by inserting different pages.

The Company Car

Wedding planning is a business in which a car is an absolute necessity. You will be driving clients to meet with vendors and visit reception venues, transporting small items, and driving to and from the wedding. All of this is next to impossible (and very expensive) to do by taxi. Your present car is the most likely candidate for the job of "company car." It doesn't have to be new, nor does it have to be an expensive and flashy model. I have never been a "car snob," and you'll find that most of your clients won't care what kind of car you drive. It does, however, have to be spotlessly clean and in good repair, as it will reflect on you and your business. If you drive a *very* old car, perhaps it is time to get a newer one. Keep the needs of your business in mind when choosing the model. A four-door car allows clients to get in and out of the back seat easily.

You may decide to have your business name on the car, although this is entirely optional. Lettering can be applied directly to the body or the window, or you may opt for a pair of magnetic signs that can be removed (preferable if you keep your present job).

Since you also use the car for personal purposes, your accountant will give you specific instructions on record-keeping. In your glove compartment, keep a log book to record your mileage. Other costs, such as repairs, insurance, and leasing are partially deductible. The more you use the car for business, the more you can deduct. Your accountant will help you come up with a reasonable ratio of personal to business use. You will read more about this in Chapter 10.

Your Portfolio

Potential clients will most likely contact you because of your advertising or your reputation. However, before they hire you, the couple will want to see what kind of work you do. Your portfolio is the best way to show them. A wedding planner's portfolio is a collection of photographs, showing past weddings. Generally, you can handle your portfolio in one of three ways:

- Keep all weddings together in a large photo album or portfolio case, in chronological order. This way, it will be ready to show at a moment's notice, although not all of the weddings will interest all clients.

- Keep all wedding photos filed in shoebox-sized containers, ready to assemble into a portfolio of a particular style of wedding, degree of formality, theme, or location. This will tailor the portfolio to a specific client, although it requires preparation before the meeting.

- Keep several smaller portfolios, each dedicated to a specific style of wedding. You will have to show several albums in order to show that you are versatile in your work.

When taking photographs at a wedding, remember that they are for your portfolio, not your family album. By all means, include some photos of the bride and groom, but concentrate on the details that you have designed—the table settings, the flowers, the cake, and the decorations.

You do not have to get permission from former clients to show these pictures. Since the portfolio has no other purpose but to be shown to perspective clients, their consent was implied when you took the pictures.

Most wedding planners frame thank-you letters from clients and hang them on the office wall. When your collection gets too large—and it will—you can store the rest in your portfolio.

Your Emergency Kit

Wedding planners carry enormous "emergency kits" that can save the day for the bride, a member of the wedding party, or even a guest. Start with the largest tote you can find. Make sure it is attractive. Mine was a floral tapestry bag, with plenty of pockets and zippered compartments.

Fill your bag with *anything* you think will come in handy during a wedding and reception. Replenish it regularly and organize it constantly. Use travel sizes to save space. Here is a beginner's list to start your emergency kit. Add to it as you see fit:

- stain remover
- Aspirin or Tylenol
- pantyhose, beige
- mini pads, tampons
- several dollars in change
- tissues
- bobby pins
- mouth wash
- pens
- gum or mints
- nail polish, clear and pink
- glue
- corsage pins
- portable steamer
- Band-Aids
- zipper-closure plastic bags
- bottled water
- lighter
- stapler
- tape
- CD of wedding music (and a CD player in the trunk of your car)
- cell phone
- extension cord
- hand lotion
- baby powder
- wet wipes

- hair spray
- magnifying glass
- nail file
- cotton balls
- travel iron
- brush and comb
- lipstick, neutral
- small sewing kit
- umbrella
- mirror
- tape measure
- small screwdriver set
- florist tape and wire

Business Failures

It may seem a little pessimistic to talk about business failures, especially so early in the book. However, by examining the reasons businesses fail, you can take steps to prevent the same thing from happening to you.

"Those who fail to plan, plan to fail." There is a great deal of truth to this popular saying. Many business owners have no plans. They feel that they can just follow along wherever the business happens to take them. If you don't make things happen, they probably won't happen. Set realistic goals and stick to them.

Many businesses fail because their owners are impatient and quit when success is just around the corner. You must start slowly and let your business grow steadily. If you have too little working capital, you will not be able to survive until your business is making money. This is a very common cause of failure. Don't overspend at the beginning; leave as much cash in reserve as possible. Have a written budget. Stick to it and revise it often.

Your business will not survive if you do not have a good knowledge of wedding planning. If you are not yet an expert, get certified and gain experience. You must also have a general knowledge of business principles and practices. The fact that you are reading this book proves that you are willing to learn what it takes to run your business.

You need a steady stream of weddings to keep the cash flowing. If it dries up, your business will not be able to survive.

The Competitive Edge

The key to success in wedding planning is to have an edge over your competitors. A bride will consider several factors before hiring you. Surprisingly, cost isn't one of them.

Your Knowledge: The bride will want to work with you if she feels you are knowledgeable. Your task is to convey this to her. Many very good wedding planners have lost jobs because their clients didn't see just how much they really knew.

Her Comfort Level: You will be sharing the most important time in the bride's life. If she doesn't bond with you, you probably won't get the job.

Your Flexibility: If you are willing to listen to what the bride wants and adjust your ideas to fit her vision, you will win the job. This is not to say that you should avoid sharing your point of view—in fact, she will want to hear it. But the bottom line is this: it's *her* wedding, and she will be eternally grateful if you can help her get what she wants.

Quality of Your Work: A bride will want to see examples of your work. Show her your portfolio so that she can see how well you coordinate small details.

Testimonials from Former Clients: Brides expect to hear good things about you from your past clients. Perhaps you have been referred by a friend; if not, show her your collection of thank-you notes.

Business Start-up Checklist

- Choose a business name and do a search to be sure it is not already in use
- Decide whether you will operate as a sole proprietorship, partnership, or corporation
- Register your business name
- Apply for tax permits
- Conduct a market analysis

- Decide whether you want a home-based business or commercial office space (see Chapter 4)

- Locate the space, plan, and decorate it

- Obtain necessary insurance coverage

- Begin acquiring office equipment

- Order business cards and letterhead

- Devise a start-up budget and determine if you will need any additional funding

- Write your business plan

- Apply for a business loan, if necessary

- Develop a marketing and advertising plan

- Design a brochure

- Locate a good accountant and lawyer

Professional Associations

There are many associations that cater to the wedding professional. Joining one of these has both pros and cons. On the plus side, you will receive a quarterly newsletter, discounts on their convention registration, recognition on their Web site, and a membership certificate. On the downside, high membership fees must be renewed yearly.

I took these factors into consideration when I formed the *Sandcastles Institute of Wedding Planning*. The membership fee is nominal, and there is no renewal, *ever*. We don't have annual conventions (I was never able to leave my busy schedule long enough to attend a convention), but we do offer a certificate, Web site recognition, quarterly online newsletter, and a ten percent discount on our services.

Visit the Institute online at *www.sandcastlesinstitute.sharibeck.com*. You may join as a certified or non-certified member, and those who attain certification are automatically upgraded.

Don't overlook your local business organizations. Start with the Board of Trade or Chamber of Commerce in your area. Advertising is available in their newsletters, and their networking meetings may be a goldmine of contacts.

Numerous associations support small business or home business. These can be found in your local newspaper, and may be worth your investigation.

For Your Notes

2

WORKING WITH CLIENTS

Setting Your Fees

Most wedding planners set their fees in one of four ways:

- flat fee
- package
- percentage of the total wedding costs
- hourly

A flat fee is exactly as its name implies. After you meet the bride and groom and discuss their needs, you will quote them a flat fee which includes all of the services they require from you. At the beginning, you may be working for substantially less to gain experience. As you progress, you can and should charge more. Until you are more experienced it may be difficult to judge what the job entails and how much your flat fee should be. It is best to break the wedding down into smaller pieces. Make a list of each task and set a dollar figure to it; refer to the list when pricing a wedding.

The second method, packaging, is quite similar. After putting together your itemized list, assemble the most popular combinations into packages. You might like to start with three packages, offering full wedding-planning services, a rehearsal/wedding day coordination, and something in between. Your fees should be all-inclusive; don't charge for every telephone call. The only exception is a travel fee that you may charge clients who are outside your geographic area.

With the percentage method, you will charge ten to fifteen percent of the total cost of the wedding as your fee for the planning involved. This method has several flaws. Although it is advantageous for a large wedding, there is just as much detailed planning involved for a smaller affair. If you plan to charge a percentage, the large and small weddings will even out.

Charge an hourly rate to couples who are planning their own weddings, but want to consult with you. It would be extremely difficult to charge this way for planning an entire wedding. Not only would you have a hard time keeping track of all the hours, but the cost of all those hours would triple the fees that you can reasonably charge.

Many wedding planners use a combination of hourly fees and packages. Their packages cover everything, but they also consult by the hour. When you have decided how you will charge, be consistent. Otherwise, you will get a reputation for charging different people in different ways, a practice that will raise eyebrows among perspective clients.

How will you present your fees? Some wedding planners set up an initial appointment at no charge to present their services and explain their fees. Others will discuss their fees over the telephone. I achieved good results by posting my fees on my Web site and including them in my brochure. I got fewer calls from brides looking for prices, and more calls from brides wanting to book my services!

Now that you have set your fees, how will you collect them? Again, protect your reputation by being consistent with all of your clients. The letter of agreement or contract will spell out what you expect in terms of payment. They will include the following:

- your total fee
- deposit (and when it is payable)
- balance (and when it is payable)
- services included in the fee

Most wedding planners ask for a fifty percent deposit upon the signing of the contract. Until you have received it, you cannot promise to reserve the date. If a client complains about the amount of the deposit, explain that it not only holds the date, but covers your expenses and the work you are doing on their behalf. Mention such things as gas and long-distance telephone calls, as well as your time.

If the fee is large and fifty percent is more than the clients can afford, you may agree to divide it into thirds, with one third due upon signing, one third due at the half-way point, and the balance due before the wedding. Be sure to specify this in the contract.

It's always best to have the client and vendor deal directly with one another. Some wedding planners contract the vendors and are billed by them. They in turn bill the client. If you decide to work this way, be sure your deposits are covered by the deposits you receive. Otherwise, you could end up with a cash flow problem. Remember that if the vendor has the contract with you, you will be responsible for payment if the client defaults. We will discuss this further in Chapter 11.

Don't be afraid to share a little before you've been hired. If you offer to look something up for a bride, you just might develop a rapport that will guarantee the job will be yours. If a caller asks for a service you don't provide, recommend someone who does. They'll find out who referred them and they'll reciprocate some day.

New wedding planners are often unsure how much to charge. Researching other wedding planners won't help—there are just too many varying figures. There is a big difference between running your own business and working for someone else. You will not have many weeks in which you can find forty billable hours because part of your work will be administrative.

So how can you determine your fee? Imagine that you are in a job you hate, making $20,800 per year, and decide to become a wedding planner. The first thing you want is a higher salary, but we will use your present salary since it gives me nice round numbers to use as an example!

> $20,800 divided by 52 weeks equals $400 per week
> $400 divided by 5 days equals $80 per day
> $80 divided by 8 hours equals $10 per hour

This is how much you made at your former job. In order to make $20,800 as a self-employed wedding planner you must multiply this by 2.5, which means that you will charge $25 per hour. The extra $15 per hour will compensate for the loss of a guaranteed forty-hour work week. As a rule, most self-employed people can bill approximately twenty-five hours per week to clients. If you take a two-week holiday, you will be billing twenty-five hours per week for fifty weeks, which at $25 per hour translates to $31,250 per year.

Next, consider your expenses. If you run your business from home, your expenses will be considerably lower. We will estimate them at $2,200 per month, or $26,400 per year. This includes a $1,600 monthly salary for you. From your billable estimate of $31,250 deduct $26,400 for expenses. This will leave you with a profit of $4,850 in addition to your $20,800 salary. Use these figures to formulate your estimated operating budget for next year. You can add an extra $400 per month to your paycheck, based on this year's actual figures, raising your income to $24,000 per year. Put the remaining $50 profit toward something for your office.

$31,250 works out to just under $2,605 per month, and $601 per week. Imagine that you have a month in which you will be working on two weddings, one of which will pay you a fee of $1,800. For the other, you have agreed to handle the flowers and the cake, and to coordinate the wedding day, for a fee of $650. You have also booked seven hours of consultation at $25 per hour. You have already made $2,625. If you plan fifteen weddings in a year for $1,800 each, you will make $27,000.

You will get a great deal of work planning bits and pieces of weddings. These amounts can add up quite quickly. For example, if you charge $300 for a wedding day coordination, two weddings a month will add up to $7,200 per year.

Now that you have the formula for determining your fees, insert your own figures into the equation. When you are just starting out, you may decide that you can accept a lower salary. Or, you may work in an affluent area that will enable you to charge higher fees. Remember, too, that your expenses will be partly compensated by the fact that you will be claiming more tax deductions.

Occasionally, you may be asked to perform jobs that are not in your contract. For example, the bride may ask you to go to her fittings and give her your opinion. Do not to charge her for this; it's all a part of adding value to your services. However, you may have been told that the flowers were already planned, only to find that you are expected to handle this. Gently explain to your clients that you will have to make a change to the contract, including the fee structure. Alternatively, you can agree to consult on an hourly basis.

For convenience, yours and the clients', gather several of your services together into a collection of packages. These should cost slightly less than the same services priced separately. Please feel free to adapt the packages that I have developed, which I present here.

Sample Pricing

This list is an example of pricing that breaks down the wedding-planning process into smaller tasks. By pricing each of these tasks, you can come up with a fair way to charge clients who do not need your complete wedding-planning service.

- Consultation, per hour $—

- Obtain estimates from caterers for clients' approval, retain caterer, and handle communication with them, $—

- Coordinate the rehearsal, wedding ceremony, and reception, $—

- Obtain estimates from the various vendors, meet with them and the clients, arrange deliveries, and handle communication, charged for *each* vendor, $—

- Traveling fee for weddings over 100 kilometers/60 miles outside our business area, $—

Sample of the Platinum Package

- Unlimited consultation, on such subjects as wedding style, degree of formality, wording of invitations, music for the ceremony, wording of wedding vows, etc.

- Develop a detailed budget

- Create a detailed task list and calendar, updated regularly

- Consultation as to the reception menu, and estimate the amount needed of liquor, beer, wine, and champagne

- Obtain estimates from caterers for your approval, retain caterer, and handle communication with them

- Contact rental business for tables, chairs, linens, etc, to arrange delivery and pickup, and to determine which items must be rented

- Consultation as to your preferences in photography, retain photographer and/or videographer approved by you, and work out a list of required shots

- Consultation as to your preferences in reception music, retain DJ approved by you, and work out a list of required songs

- Consultation as to your preferences in flowers, retain a florist approved by you, and work out a list of flowers needed

- Obtain estimates from bakers for your approval, retain baker, and handle communication with them regarding the wedding cake

- Communicate with the vendors on your behalf

- Assistance in finding clergy to officiate at the wedding, if you are not affiliated with a particular church

- Development of a schedule of vendor deposits, payments and balances due, updated regularly

- Be on hand at the rehearsal, and assist with the same
- Develop a wedding-day itinerary
- Supervision of set-up, flower arrangement, etc., at the ceremony site
- Assist you and wedding party prior to the ceremony
- Supervise the line-up for the processional
- Remove small items from the ceremony site and transport to the reception site
- Supervise the set-up of the reception site
- Place centerpieces and place cards
- Receive deliveries on your behalf (wedding cake, flowers, etc.)
- Supervision and communication with the vendors throughout the reception
- Assist your guests in any way possible, and handle anything unexpected
- Return of rental items, if applicable
- Issue payments to vendors

Sample of the Gold Package

- Unlimited consultations by telephone, e-mail, or in person
- Develop a wedding budget
- Develop a detailed task list and calendar, updated regularly
- Locate and contract up to five (5) vendors or services approved by you
- Work with you and the vendors as to your preferences and needs
- Communicate with the vendors on your behalf
- Develop a schedule of vendor deposits, payments and balance due dates, updated regularly
- Be present at your rehearsal, and assist with same
- Develop a wedding day itinerary
- Supervise the set-up of the ceremony site, floral arrangements, etc.
- Assist you and the wedding party prior to the ceremony

- Supervise the line-up of the wedding party prior to the processional
- Transport small items from the ceremony to the reception
- Receive deliveries on your behalf (wedding cake, flowers, etc.)
- Supervise the set-up of the reception site
- Place centerpieces and place cards
- Issue payments to the vendors
- Assist your guests whenever possible, and handle anything unexpected
- Supervision and communication with vendors for the duration of the reception
- Return rental items, if applicable

Sample of the Silver Package

- Up to three consultations, in which the wedding plans will be discussed in detail
- Preparation of a detailed itinerary of the wedding day
- Supervision of the set up of the ceremony site, flower arrangement, etc
- Assistance to the bride and wedding party prior to the ceremony
- Transportation of small items from the ceremony to the reception
- Supervision of the set-up of the reception site
- Placement of centerpieces, place cards, etc
- Receiving deliveries on your behalf (wedding cake, flowers, etc)
- Supervision of and communication with vendors for the duration of the reception
- Assistance to the guests in any way possible, and the handling of anything unexpected
- Issue payment to vendors

Cancellation and Postponement Policies

Develop a policy that you will follow if the wedding is canceled or postponed. In this situation, most vendor deposits will be lost. If you hold a date open for your clients, and even turn down other weddings because you are committed to them, you are entitled to compensation. Your contract or letter of agreement will state that the deposit is nonrefundable. However, each situation is unique. If the wedding is cancelled due to the death or serious illness of the bride and groom, most wedding planners choose to be compassionate and refund the deposit. Check the facts first, though, as this is a common way to get a refund after a broken engagement.

Many wedding planners and vendors handle a postponement the same way. Some are willing to simply change the date; others will demand a new deposit. I always preferred to change the date. What you may lose in doing this small favor will be made up in referrals. If you are already booked on the new date, the couple will forfeit their deposit and the contract is terminated.

Motivating the Bride

Often, the bride has no idea what she wants, so how can the wedding planner lead her to it? By simply understanding what motivates the bride, you may be able to figure it out before she does!

The bride needs a combination of value, benefit, and emotion. If you can give these to her, you will be able to help her plan the wedding of her dreams. Since the average bride is not consciously aware of this, you will probably be unsuccessful in explaining it to her. But when you start to fulfill these needs, you'll be surprised just how quickly she responds!

Motivating the bride takes practice. You must be able to read between the lines when she is talking to you. Learn to state facts in a way that will trigger an emotional response, while at the same time be perceived as a benefit. By hiring you to plan her wedding, the bride will save time—that is a benefit. Hiring you will give her more time to spend with her fiancé. That is a benefit with the added power of emotion!

Benefit Selling

As unromantic as it sounds, the purpose of your first meeting with a bride and groom will be to sell yourself, your services, and your expertise. Take the time to familiarize yourself with the basics of selling. Note that I tend to emphasize the bride. Although the groom's opinion is important, if you win the bride you will usually win the job.

Perhaps you are not the only wedding planner they are considering. How can you be sure you'll be the one they hire? By using a technique called "benefit selling." Simply put, you promise the client a benefit. If you have benefits that the competition does not, use them in all of your advertising and personal interviews. If not, create some.

Give the couple the impression that *you* are the preferred choice. Sell yourself. The pressures of planning a wedding, working full-time, and still finding time for each other have made today's couples more aware of the kinds of services they want. Remember, these are *perceived* benefits. Find a need and fill it. Create a need based on some of these benefits:

- You will save money

- You will save time

- You will save energy because I will be doing the legwork for you

- You will leave the unglamorous details of your wedding planning to me, so that you can concentrate on each other

- You will get better service if you meet the wedding vendors through me

- You will take advantage of my many years of wedding-planning experience

- You will avoid costly mistakes

- You will have the wedding of your dreams without the nightmares

- You will be relaxed throughout the wedding-planning process

- You will not have overlooked any details

- You will have me at your disposal

- All your wedding dreams will come true

Focus on the bride, not yourself. Notice the wording of the benefits: "You will save time," not "I will save you time."

Emotional Selling

Create an emotional response in the bride, and she will be more likely to hire you. She will feel that she just has to have what only you can give her. In the wedding business we work with emotion every day. Include it in your advertising and in your meetings with clients. Wedding talk gives every bride the "warm fuzzies," even if she is the CEO of a Fortune 500 company.

How do you convey emotion in your business? Use some of these words and phrases:

- The most important day of your life
- The beginning of your lives together
- The perfect wedding
- Romance is in the air
- Fairy-tale wedding
- A day to remember
- A dream come true
- Once in a lifetime
- Exquisite

Although the bride wants the best, she will never buy from a company claiming to be the best. No one trusts a claim like that. The secret is "perception." Because of the emotions you invoke in the bride, she will perceive you to be the best. Always remember, *subtle implication is better than blatant specification.* Imply that you are the best wedding planner for the job (which of course you are!) and the bride will pick up your emotional message. She will just have to have you plan her wedding so that she can fulfill her dreams on the most important day of her life!

Buying Signals

Many signs will indicate that the bride is ready to hire you. Look for non-verbal body language:

- She will nod her head in agreement as you speak.
- If her legs are crossed, they will be facing you.

- She will absentmindedly reach for her purse or her checkbook.

- She will lean forward.

- Her mouth will be relaxed.

- She will make calculations on paper.

- She will rest her hands on her chin.

You can also pick up signs by what she says. She will agree with whatever you say, and ask you questions. She will ask how much deposit you need, and when the balance is due. She will say things like, "When you take us to see the florist ..."

Overcoming Objections

Before you can sign the contract, you must help the bride over any objections that remain. If the bride answers with "yes, but ..." she has objections that can be successfully resolved. If you can manage this, you will be the one she will choose to plan her wedding. With practice, you should be able to turn any objection around and make it a reason why you are right for the job.

The main objection is likely to be the cost of hiring a wedding planner. Explain that you are able to *save* her money, as well as keep her within the wedding budget.

Perhaps she wants to plan her own wedding (why is she speaking to you?) but what she is actually saying is that she is afraid to give control to someone else. Assure her that she and her fiancé are very much in control. No decisions will be made unless they are made by the couple. You will offer the bride suggestions and lead her to vendors, but she is still the boss.

Maybe her mother has everything under control. Don't try to tell her that her mother might not be the most competent person to plan her wedding. Instead, offer to help her mother by providing hourly consultations at intervals throughout the wedding-planning process, followed by the coordination of the wedding day.

Maybe the bride wants to hire you, but the groom thinks wedding planners are unnecessary. Explain to him that hiring a wedding planner is the same as having an accountant do your taxes. A professional can avoid the pitfalls that the average person is unaware of. As well, you can give the bride more free time to spend with him.

Perhaps the bride assumes that the caterer will handle everything and she doesn't need you. Remind her that the caterer will not help her with the flowers, time the speeches and toasts, or be sure that her elderly grandmother gets special treatment. These jobs all fall on you.

Closing the Sale

To use sales jargon, when the bride and groom are ready to sign the contract, you have closed the sale. Eventually you will intuitively know which close will work for which bride. In the meantime, here are some to practice:

- At the beginning of the meeting, the bride may have her resistance up. Remove it by asking her to wait until afterwards to make her decision. Tell her you just want to explain how you can help her with her wedding plans, and then *she* can tell *you* whether she needs you. Ask her questions that will allow you to tailor your service to her needs, and she will be sure to hire you.

- Ask a series of questions to which the bride will answer "yes." It is then harder to say "no." Some questions to ask are, "Do you want to save money planning your wedding?" "Do you want to have a stress-free engagement?" "Do you want your wedding to be all you ever dreamed of?" Word your questions in such a way that "no" is not an optional answer.

- Use questions throughout the meeting to get feedback. Stop and ask, "Is that what you were thinking of?" "Are we thinking of the same thing?" "Do you agree?" The bride will be amazed at how you can practically read her mind.

- Use imagery. By planting images in the bride's mind, you are giving her mental possession and she doesn't want to let it go. She knows that you can make it hers in reality.

All of these methods will take practice. Don't try to be someone you're not. Be natural, honest and totally yourself. You may have to work on a combination of closes. Don't push the bride, lead her. Don't give up. Over ninety percent of all clients say "yes" only after they've said "no" at least four times. More than forty percent of consultants give up after the first "no."

Initial Consultation

Although you and the bride may end up doing much of the planning alone, your first meeting will include the groom. His input is important. In fact, I once had a groom who did more of the planning than the bride! Don't be surprised if the groom leaves much of the decision-making to his fiancée. Most men aren't into small details, but they know how much the bride enjoys the planning process!

The initial consultation can take place at your office, the home of the bride or groom (or their shared home), or at another location. Meeting at their home is probably the quickest way to get to know your clients' tastes and personal styles. Or, you may decide to meet for coffee at a spot half-way between.

Be punctual. In fact, be a little early. It is not proper to show up at a private home more than five minutes early; your hosts may be doing a last-minute cleaning.

Answer their questions. Dispel any myths they may have heard about wedding planners. You are not going to tell them what they should have at their wedding. *They* are going to tell *you*, and you are going to help them get it.

In your briefcase, have a file you started, based on your telephone or e-mail contact. Get a feeling for the wedding by asking questions. What is the budget? What are their preferences? Are there divorced parents you need to work around?

If you have followed the selling techniques in this chapter, the couple may be ready to sign a contract or letter of agreement and give you a deposit. If they need more time to think about it, be sure to follow up not more than two days later.

The Contract

You and your clients will sign either a contract or a letter of agreement. A letter of agreement will usually suffice, but for a large or complicated job a contract seems a little more formal. Both are legally binding.

You may wish to draw up a generic contract which you can change to suit the circumstances of each individual wedding. Have your lawyer review the contract to be sure you have protected yourself well. The formal contract will most likely contain the following:

The date of the wedding and the parties to the contract.

A list of your obligations to the couple, itemized.

A clause that reads like: "*Sandcastles'* role will be that of advisor and consultant. The bride and groom reserve the right to make the final decisions, which *Sandcastles* will implement." In other words, you will advise the couple on such things as caterers, florists, and photographers, but they are responsible for making the final choice. This reassures the clients that they are in control of their own wedding, and subtly lets them know that they assume the responsibility that comes with this kind of control.

The method of charging, initial deposit, installments, and final payment.

Cease-work clause: Although this sounds rather harsh, wedding planners do a great deal of free work for their clients. This clause will reinforce the fact that payments must be prompt. Choose a reasonable grace period (such as seven to ten business days) for each installment, after which you will cease to work on the wedding.

Cancellation cause: Occasionally, it may be necessary to terminate the contract, such as if the wedding is cancelled. Spell out your refund policies carefully. As a general rule, the deposit is nonrefundable. It is kept by you in compensation for work already done and in case you are unable to rebook the date.

Postponement clause: If the wedding will go ahead but the date will be changed, state your policies.

No-fault clause: The clients will acknowledge that you are an independent business, in no way affiliated with the vendors, and that you will not be held liable for any acts, errors, or omissions on their part. Keep in mind that this clause may not hold up in court if you have formed an alliance with a vendor by accepting a commission or finder's fee.

Changes to the contract: These *must* be made in writing and signed or initialed by all parties to the contract. That way, clients cannot add something without your knowledge and then insist that you deliver on it. If the changes are numerous, they will be added to the contract as a separate sheet of paper known as an "exhibit." If only a couple of changes are needed, they can be made right on the contract.

Legal fees: If a dispute should end up in court will the winner collect legal fees? If so, it must be stated in the contract.

Signatures to the contract: The contract must be dated and signed by you, the bride, and the groom. An initial line should be added at the bottom of all pages, including the exhibits. You and the clients initial each page.

The actual wording of the contract is up to you. Again, you are advised to have your lawyer look over everything before you sign. To keep it legal, there are certain things that *must* be in every contract:

1. Offer: The services that you are offering to provide.

2. Acceptance: Obviously, if the client doesn't accept your offer, there is no contract.

3. Consideration: Something the client promises in return for your offer. In business contracts, this takes the form of monetary compensation. The courts will not enforce an unreasonable contract, so make sure your pricing is not out of line.

4. Legality of subject: The chances of you encountering this one are slim, but for your information, a contract is not enforceable if the subject is illegal, criminal, or harmful to others.

5. Written vs. verbal: Since verbal contracts are hard to enforce, don't even consider them. Furthermore, the law states that any contract that cannot be followed within a year must be in writing; that is the case with many weddings.

The Letter of Agreement

A letter of agreement is just as legal as a contract. It is not as formally-worded, but contains many of the same components. It is preferred for a smaller wedding, wedding day coordination, or the planning of several details only. Here are some of the components of a letter of agreement:

1. The first page will be on your letterhead; any additional pages will be on blank sheets.

2. The letter is addressed to the bride.

3. There is a reference to the groom by name, the wedding date, and perhaps a recent telephone call.

4. There is a detailed, itemized list of everything the job is to cover.

5. There is a quote for the entire fee, a request for a deposit, details of installment payments, and a date for final payment

6. There is a no-fault clause, as detailed in the previous section. Even if the client contracts the vendors, you are wise to use this clause.

7. There is a clause stating that all changes must be made in writing and initialed by all parties.

8. The cancellation and postponement policies are clearly spelled out.

9. The request for the couple to sign and date the letter, return it with a check, and a reminder to make the check payable to your business name.

10. I like a warm sentiment to close, something like "I look forward to working with you to make your wedding day the most memorable of your life."

11. Signatures

Turning Down a Job

"Why," you ask, "would I ever turn down a wedding?" As long as you are not already booked for the same day, you will probably never want to turn down work. However, there are situations which may result in you doing just that.

You may find yourself alone with the groom, who is acting inappropriately. If you feel that you are unable to work with him, you will not be able to do a good job planning his wedding. Likewise, if a couple asks you to do something illegal or unethical, you may not feel that you can enter into a business relationship with them.

I once had a bride contact me about coordinating her wedding day; her future mother-in-law would be doing all the planning. During our initial telephone conversation, she told me that the groom was so pleased that she was going to hire me, because—and I quote, "now he will have someone to yell at when things go wrong!" Needless to say, I did not take the job!

Although honesty is the best policy, sometimes tact is better. You don't want to be the one to tell someone that her fiancé made a pass at you, or accuse someone of being unethical.

In this case, a little white lie may be best. Listen to what they say at your meeting, and then tell them that you have another party interested in the same date. Explain that you must give them first chance at that date (which is the truth). A couple of days later, call and tell them that the other party has signed the letter of agreement, wish them well, and you're off the hook.

Please understand, though, that this is the *only* time you can ever justify anything but absolute truth to your clients!

Free Consultations and Free Services

If you plan to offer free consultations, you must be careful to do just *that*. A common marketing ploy is to have the bride show up for a free consultation, only to give her a sales pitch.

A bride who is meeting you for a free consultation will probably have a list of questions to ask you, or perhaps she would like you to look over her budget. She will be very unhappy if you ignore her questions and try instead to convince her that she needs you to plan her wedding. She will come away from the meeting disillusioned, and will be even less likely to hire you than she was before.

On the other hand, a free consultation can be the perfect way for the bride to discover just how much she needs you. As you answer her questions, she will be impressed with the way you are able to visualize the wedding and reception, and she will be grateful for your expert advice. The time may come when she will have more questions, or perhaps she will realize that she needs professional help. Guess who she'll call?

Over the years, I have received occasional telephone calls or e-mails from complete strangers asking questions related to their weddings. I always took the time to answer and offer a few additional suggestions. It took perhaps five minutes of my time, and more than one of the callers eventually became clients.

Many wedding planners who are just starting out will offer their services to family and friends in order to get experience and portfolio pictures. This is usually done without charge and is a win/win situation. The wedding planner gets a chance to meet with vendors who will become her business allies. The bride benefits from having her wedding planned by a talented new professional.

On the downside, human nature dictates that we tend to value things higher if we have to pay for them. Therefore, be sure to call this a "complimentary service" instead of "free." Besides, there really *is* a payment for the service—a glowing testimonial and pictures of the wedding. If you are particularly close to the bride and groom, you may wish to make this your wedding gift to them.

If you do not know the couple well, it may be preferable to charge a small fee. There is a great deal of work for a beginner to handle, and some form of payment should be in order. Determine in writing what your responsibilities are. That will eliminate the possibility that they may try to take advantage of the situation.

The Add-on Sale

Opportunities to make an add-on sale in the wedding-planning business are not very obvious, but there happen to be many. Take stock of your other interests and talents. Many wedding planners make or sell wedding-related items:

- silk flower arrangements
- silk flower bouquets
- ring pillows
- flower girl baskets
- unity candles
- plume pens
- toasting glasses
- invitations

Some provide a service:

- invitation calligraphy
- cake decorating
- hall decorating
- flower arranging
- car decorating

Many own items that they are willing to rent:

- columns
- candelabra and candlesticks
- punchbowls
- silver trays
- topiary trees

Give a Little Extra

Everything you do to please your clients will pay off in referrals and word-of-mouth advertising. This is secondary to the satisfaction of seeing how your hard work and attention to detail has created the perfect wedding. There are many ways to give your clients that little extra:

- A bride may be too shy to mention any small changes she may wish to make. If you give her the opportunity, she will be eternally grateful.

- Always "go the second mile." If a client asks you to find two harpists for her to audition, locate three.

- Be available on weekends and in the evening. Be willing to drive to the clients' home instead of expecting them to come to you.

- Don't be a clock watcher. Unless you have another appointment, don't cut a client's telephone call or meeting short.

- Be willing to offer advice, even if you haven't been hired to do so. If a bride asks you for the name of a good bridal salon, pass on the information.

- Don't "nickel and dime" your clients. Gas, long distance telephone calls, and photocopies should be built into your fees, never itemized and charged.

- Go out of your way to make wedding guests feel comfortable. Frequently scan the room, and offer to help anyone in any way you can.

- Send a card to the couple on their first wedding anniversary.

- Be a good listener. Pay as much attention to what your clients are *not* saying as to what they are saying.

- *Never* try to get your clients to spend more money. Instead, try to get them the most for their wedding-planning dollars.

- Always be punctual for meetings. It shows the other person that you value their time.

- Try to have your regular vendors do something extra for your clients. After all, you represent repeat business.

- Always admit when you are wrong and try to find a solution.

Don't worry that giving extra to your clients will cause them to take advantage of you. No one can take advantage of you without your permission. Know when to give, but also know when to dig in your heels.

Client Feedback

All successful businesses rely on feedback from their customers and clients. We welcome positive feedback, and yet we dread negative feedback. Positive feedback tells us what we are doing right so we can keep doing it. But negative feedback is actually more useful. People tend to get defensive when they feel that they are being insulted or criticized. Try to get over these initial feelings and look at what the client is really saying. What is the complaint? Is it well-founded? Can you use it as a springboard for future improvement?

As you are planning a wedding, stop at midpoint and do a "reality check." Remember that a client's perception of your service is based on expectations. Make sure you deliver more than they expect.

Never take it personally if a client turns down one of your ideas. It doesn't mean that there's anything wrong with the idea, only that it's not right for them.

When the newlyweds have returned from their honeymoon, mail them a follow-up survey. It is easy to check off multiple-choice answers without much thought, so you may find open-ended questions are more revealing. You will get a better response rate if you enclose a self-addressed stamped envelope. Following are examples of open-ended questions. Use or adapt these for your surveys:

1. How willing are you to recommend us?

2. What did you appreciate most about our service?

3. How accessible were we if you needed to get a hold of us?

4. How would you rate our knowledge of wedding planning on a scale of one to ten?

5. In your opinion, did we deliver what we promised?

6. How well did we understand you, your ideas, and your needs?

7. How many wedding planners did you try before calling us?

8. How satisfied were you with the way we treated your family and guests?

Here are the same questions, in multiple-choice format:

1. How willing are you to recommend us?

    a.   Very willing

    b.   Not very willing

2. What did you appreciate most about our service?

    a.   Your knowledge

    b.   Your ability to put us at ease

    c.   Your organizational skills

    d.   Your people skills

    e.   All of the above

3. How accessible were we if you needed to get a hold of us?

    a.   Very accessible

    b.   Somewhat accessible

    c.   Not at all accessible

4. How would you rate our knowledge of wedding planning?

    a.   0-2

    b.   3-5

    c.   6-7

    d.   8-9

    e.   10

5. In your opinion, did we deliver what we promised?

    a.   Yes

    b.   No

6. How well did we understand you, your ideas, and your needs?

    a.   Very well

    b.   Satisfactorily

    c.   Poorly

7.   How many wedding planners did you try before calling us?

   a.   Several

   b.   One

   c.   You are the only one we called

8.   How satisfied were you with the way we treated your family and guests?

   a.   Very satisfied

   b.   Somewhat satisfied

   c.   Not at all satisfied

Handling Complaints

Of course, you will keep dissatisfied brides to a minimum, but you are only human and you can't expect to please everyone all of the time. There is no such thing as a trivial complaint. By taking action, you can turn the situation around and end up with a stronger relationship with your client. A bride who is able to assert herself when she feels she has been unfairly treated will be very loyal to you when she feels you take her seriously.

If a bride should call you, angry about something you did (or didn't do), disarm her immediately by agreeing with her. You are not committing yourself to solve the problem, but you are acknowledging that there is a problem, that she has a right to be upset, and that there are solutions to this problem.

Don't try to place blame if the situation is your fault; admit you made a mistake. Don't accept the blame for someone else's mistake, but offer to come up with a solution. Listen to the complaint, acknowledge the problem, and try to solve it on the spot. If this isn't possible, tell the bride you will look into the situation and get back to her. Then do it. Never let the client lose face. Even if she's wrong, she's right.

Be kind; don't argue, lose your temper, or use a harsh tone of voice. Don't react defensively. Never say anything against your business, your suppliers, or even your competition. Concentrate on bringing the situation quickly and peacefully to an end, even if it means making a small concession for the sake of public relations.

Managing Family Dynamics

Weddings bring out the best *and* the worst in people. You may be dragged into family arguments, and it is important that you know how to tactfully handle these situations. From the start, be impartial. Under no circumstances should you take sides; someone will always end up with hurt feelings. Instead, try to be a mediator. Use your knowledge of wedding etiquette to settle disputes.

A common problem results when families try to impose their ideas and wishes onto the young couple. This problem is compounded when the bride and groom are from different cultures or religions. Add to this the fact that the parents have been dreaming of this day since their children were born. No wonder these situations become so emotional! As an outsider, it may be easier for you to sit back and see the situation objectively.

In my experience, the best way to handle this problem is to sit down with everyone involved. Have each person tell you *one* thing that they would most love to see in the wedding. Write these down, and help the bride and groom incorporate them into the ceremony or reception. Each parent and grandparent will see their fondest wish granted and the bride and groom will feel good about making this small sacrifice for the sake of the family.

Another common situation involves divorced parents and wedding pictures. They should be able to put aside their differences long enough to pose for their child's wedding pictures, but that's not always the way it is. You may be called upon to help smooth out the situation. Remind them that this is not their day, and that they should cooperate for the sake of the bride and groom. If this doesn't work, suggest that they have three pictures taken—one with Dad and his new wife for him, one of Mom and her new husband for her, and one with Mom and Dad for the bride and groom.

Most family disagreements are solved by compromise. Help the family understand that harmony can be the greatest wedding gift of all. If all else fails, they will have to agree to disagree!

The "Liberated" Bride

Many wedding customs date back to ancient times. The bride is "given away" by her father, reminiscent of marriage by purchase. The bride feeds the first piece of wedding cake to her husband as a symbol that she will continue to take care of him. The throwing of rice began as a fertility ritual. Today, we consider these to be a part of the traditional festivities.

Occasionally, however, you may encounter a bride who finds such things offensive. She may refuse to have anything to do with customs that are so "demeaning" to women.

As her wedding planner, suggest alternatives. In many cases, the traditions can be kept, but the bride can be prompted to look at them in a different way. Suggest that the bride's father escort her up the aisle to meet the groom as a way to welcome him to the family. Have the cake-cutting ceremony adjusted to reflect that the couple takes care of each other. And let the guests blow bubbles, as rice is not allowed at many churches anyway.

Your Role in the Destination Wedding

If your clients plan to travel to a far-off location for their wedding, your role will be somewhat limited. You may be asked to discuss the legalities of the wedding ceremony, recommend a travel agent, and perhaps give advice on the flowers, attire, and etiquette surrounding such a wedding. However, unless you will be traveling to the wedding destination with the couple, your involvement will end there.

It's quite another story if you plan weddings in a tourist area. Some wedding planners run their businesses in the Caribbean, Hawaii, or romantic European locations; they specialize in destination weddings.

If you don't live and work in a tourist area, perhaps you can enter into a business arrangement with a wedding planner who does, whereby you refer clients to each other. Some wedding planners have gone so far as to work in the travel industry so that they can handle the bookings as well as the wedding plans.

Testimonials

After a wedding, you can expect an e-mail or thank-you note from the bride and groom. I've even received postcards from couples on their honeymoons. These are heartwarming, and they are also valuable in securing future clients.

Hang the best in beautiful frames on your office wall; the rest can go into your portfolio. The photographs in your portfolio do not convey the intangibles—your dedication, your hard work, and your ability to please the bride. This is evident in the glowing words of the testimonials.

If a bride gives you an especially kind compliment, ask if you can quote her on that. It would make a nice addition to your Web site or brochure. Or, jokingly ask her to put it in writing—she just may!

You may occasionally be asked to provide the names and telephone numbers of past clients. If you have had an especially close rapport with a bride, ask if you can use her as a future reference. She is sure to agree to this.

For Your Notes

3

THE PSYCHOLOGY OF WEDDINGS

What *Does* the Bride Want?

Not even the bride herself knows the answer to this question! There is much going on in her mind. She is torn between choices, exhausted from emotion, and confused over so many small details.

At this time of her life, her best friend (next to the groom) is her wedding planner. In order to do your job thoroughly, you must be able to understand why the bride acts the way she does. You must be able to remain professional even when she falls apart and not take her outbursts seriously. You have to understand what she wants, because she may not be able to put her feelings into words. And, you must be able to gently guide her toward the perfect choices for her wedding.

Some brides are a delight to work with; others drive you crazy. In some cases, the bride is reacting to issues that confuse and scare her. More often, she is simply frantic with her wedding plans at a time when she must deal with highly-charged emotions.

In this chapter, we will examine a few of the personality types you will encounter among your brides. As a wedding planner, you are by no means expected to analyze the complex workings of the human mind, but if you understand what is happening to the bride it will be easier for you to deal with her. And remember, rarely do you find a bride who is a total tyrant—who would want to marry her?

The Diva

The Diva thinks that she is the most important person in the world. Now that she is getting married, she is going to outdo herself! By the time you finish working with her, you will be icing the wedding cake with Prozac! Nothing is good enough for the Diva. Although she will occasionally be pleasant, she is either condescending or angry at our inferiority. The best way to describe her is "passionate." It may help to remember that once you are on her good side, she will be fiercely loyal you.

The Diva will have to see more venues than the average bride, taste every dish the caterer offers, and expect you to be at her beck and call at all hours.

She is not so much selfish as she is self-aware. She wants the best because she feels she deserves it; she is simply making sure her needs are filled. To the Diva, this is not just a wedding. It is an extravaganza, with her in the starring role. In a very real sense, as she walks down the aisle she will be stepping onto a stage. Every detail must be perfect because her adoring public will be watching. She feels obligated to give the performance they expect from her.

The Diva is a perfectionist. If you can give her the impression that you are the *perfect* wedding planner, she will be more likely to listen to you. Guide her gently but allow her to go a little overboard. Her family and friends are probably expecting an element of surprise.

Fasten your seatbelt—the Diva will take you for a ride you will never forget! When she drives you particularly crazy, remember this: the Diva demands the best—that's why she hired you!

The Spoiled Brat

The Spoiled Brat demands and gets what she wants by throwing temper tantrums. Daddy and her fiancé give in to keep peace. The Spoiled Brat uses this to her advantage. She doesn't appreciate any favor given to her. She expects it.

The Spoiled Brat has never learned the art of give and take, a skill that is so valuable in marriage. She only gets what she wants because she demands it, not because someone has given it freely.

The Spoiled Brat may have been an only child, never having to share with anyone. Perhaps she was the youngest child, adored and indulged. She may have been the middle child, forced to speak up and demand her rights. Or, maybe she was the eldest child, bossing her younger siblings around. Now she is a bride, the center of attention. She has a captive audience and an entourage of people trying to please her. Of course, she feels that this is her due. Hopefully she'll try to be just a little charming!

As her wedding planner, how do you handle the Spoiled Brat? When she is disagreeable, look her straight in the eye and tell her that you will speak with her when she is ready to treat you with respect. After several times, she'll realize that she can't treat you the way she treats everyone else.

The Shy Bride

After the Diva and the Spoiled Brat, the Shy Bride is a breath of fresh air. That is, until you start to work with her, and then you begin to feel sorry for her. Here is a girl who would much rather sit in the congregation, but who must walk down the aisle with every eye on her. No wonder she's so emotional!

The Shy Bride may not be so much an introvert as simply a private person. She may genuinely dislike commotion and find it embarrassing to receive attention from others. She is likely to take things very seriously. She considers her wedding vows to be much more important than the lavish party afterward. A quiet, private wedding ceremony may work best for her, followed by a reception for those who did not attend the ceremony.

Often, a Shy Bride will blossom after the wedding and become a self-assured individual. Consider Princess Diana at her wedding to Prince Charles. "Shy Di" would become the most photographed woman in the world, but there were times during her wedding ceremony when she was visibly uncomfortable. Your bride is feeling the same way, although on a much smaller scale.

Don't allow anyone to gush over this bride; she needs space. Simplicity is often the key. This is a girl who will not feel comfortable in a large bridal salon with salespeople fussing over her. Arrange for her to work quietly with her mother and one salesperson. Narrow down the choices ahead of time to avoid overwhelming her. If you work gently with her, she should be fine by the time her big day arrives.

The Ambivalent Bride

The Ambivalent Bride has no idea what she wants. This is probably the reason she hired you! She changes her mind daily, or even hourly. It is a big step for her to have made up her mind to get married in the first place!

Why is she this way? Because she wants to have everything perfect. By choosing one thing, she has to turn her back on something else. She is filled with nagging doubts that she may have made the wrong choice. These doubts become so overwhelming that she cannot control them. It is at this moment that she will call and ask you to change the menu for the umpteenth time. Procrastination is her way of avoiding a decision. If she waits too long, venues and vendors may already be booked, so she'll have fewer from which to choose. That way, a wrong choice won't be *her* mistake.

The Ambivalent Bride enjoys this even less than you do. Her inability to make a decision is difficult on her. Sit down, look her in the eye, and explain that she can't have *everything*; she has to narrow down her choices. Remind her that this is why she hired you. Then, present her with your recommendations. Be firm; steer her toward a decision. Once the nonrefundable deposit has been made, she may feel less inclined to change her mind. Praise her on having made such a wise choice. Remember, positive reinforcement is the key!

The Hostile Bride

This is the bride who has hired you to help plan her wedding, but who obviously doesn't want you around. She turns down your ideas and makes you feel like an intruder. Before you take it personally, look at the Hostile Bride's situation.

She sees her wedding as the most important day of her life, and hires you because she has no idea how to make it perfect. Your competence in an area in which she feels awkward causes resentment. You are the one with control over *her* special day.

You are caught in a vicious circle. The more you try to help her, the more she will resent your expertise. At all times, impress upon this bride that she is the boss. Ask for her direction, such as, "Who would you like me to call first, the florist or the photographer?" Always make her think that your ideas are her own.

The Bride with Control Issues

The bride who has control issues is easy to spot. Her wedding plans have created chaos in her well-organized life. She doesn't seem to have too much control anymore, yet she is trying to control everyone around her.

There are two types of controlling brides. The first is a cousin to the Diva, but without the gigantic ego. She has always been a "control freak," but now that she's getting married she tries to boss everyone around. Her bridesmaids can never do enough for her. She makes them feeling guilty if they dare to say "no" to any of her outrageous requests. To make matters worse, she tries to tell you and the vendors how to do your jobs!

Unfortunately, nothing can be done for this bride. Advise her friends, family, and bridesmaids to dig in their heels when she asks for something unreasonable.

After a few firm refusals, she should get the message. She'll settle into her regular controlling pattern after the wedding.

The second is grasping onto *anything* that she can control. She is reacting to fears, such as fear of change, fear of commitment, fear of losing her independence, or fear of the unknown. She feels that she is losing control of her life, and tries to compensate by over-controlling.

Let her know you understand. Tell her every bride feels this way, and it will pass. Other than that, let her be. She'll be just fine after the wedding.

The Bride with Money Issues

Money issues usually have deep-seated psychological causes. They often stem from an unfounded fear of being destitute, or a need to buy objects to compensate for something that is missing. Your job is not to analyze the bride, but to gently help her understand that it is necessary to control overspending or loosen the purse strings.

The penny pincher is afraid to spend money. We are not talking about the bride who wants to be sure she is getting the most for her wedding-planning dollars. Rather, we are talking about the bride who wants you to plan a sit-down prime rib reception for two hundred and fifty guests at an exclusive country club, and insists that it can be done on a $2,000 budget—yes, it *has* happened to me! The secret is to try to get her used to a series of small expenses, so that the larger ones won't send her into shock.

The spendthrift is quite the opposite: she can't wait to spend money and a wedding gives her the perfect excuse. However, an unlimited wedding budget is not the dream-come-true that it seems to be. Wedding plans can go awry very quickly if the bride is buying items that don't fit into the overall scheme. It is helpful to have a monetary limit in order to narrow down choices and make it easier for the bride to make decisions.

There is no need for parents (or the couple who are paying for their own wedding) to go overboard and end up in debt. The nicest weddings are within the means of those who are paying the bills. Remind your clients that they have no one to impress but themselves.

For Your Notes

4

SETTING UP YOUR OFFICE

Home or Office?

One of the first decisions you must make is whether to rent office space or start your business in your home. Wedding planning lends itself well to the home office trend. There are many reasons why renting office space may not be worthwhile. You will be spending many hours away from the office, and many of your in-office hours will be spent alone. Meetings with clients are often at their homes or at the wedding site.

Consider the pros and cons before you open your home to your business.

Do you really want your home to be disrupted by the business? How does your husband feel? Your children? Do you want your clients to know where you live? Will they drop by at any time because they know you'll be there? Do you live in an upscale neighborhood and think that your clients will question your fees because you can afford such a nice home? Or, do you live in a modest home and worry that they may not see what good taste you really have? Are you willing to clean up before clients come over? Will you lose business because there is no sign outside?

Before you sign a lease on an office space, consider the good points of working from home. Do you like to go over your notes while still in your bathrobe? Do you like the idea of walking down the hall to work instead of commuting? Do you want to use your home to showcase your creative talents? Do you want to begin your business without a large rent payment every month? Would you like a big tax write-off?

When I started *Sandcastles* the disadvantages were not a problem for me. My home is not intimidating, nor is it too simple for my more affluent clients. Although I live in a three-bedroom condominium, I have decorated my home in eighteenth-century elegance. I have always been a well-organized person and at any given moment my home is tidy enough for clients. My husband and my daughter were very supportive. Best of all, I could even work by the pool!

If you are thinking of an office away from home, consider the neighborhood. Remember the saying, "location, location, location." Weddings are often associated with money; your business will be better suited to a more affluent area. Of course, this means higher rent. Have your lawyer look over the lease before you sign anything. This is called "due diligence," and it's smart business.

If your office will be at home, have a space set aside exclusively for your business; a corner of the family room will not do. Make it as professional as possible, and try to have it close to the entrance of your home. That way, clients won't be walking halfway through your house to get to the office. Choose a space with good lighting, a phone jack, storage, and adequate electrical outlets.

The main advantage is also the biggest disadvantage—you are at home. It is very difficult for some women to draw the line between wife/mother time and office time. Add to this the neighbor who always drops by, and you can see how you have to be exceptionally well-disciplined to get any work done.

If you have small children, you cannot ignore their needs. They may be one of the reasons you decided on a home-based business in the first place. On the other hand, the business is important to the financial well-being of your family. Balancing their needs and those of the business may be a matter of adjusting your schedule. Return telephone calls while the kids are napping, as it is impossible to sound professional with young children in the background. Arrange a play time for them at a friend's home, and reciprocate at a time when you are not "in the office." If they have no playmates nearby, they may benefit from a half-day of preschool.

Housework is another problem. It nags at the back of your mind. Be sure to set strict office hours, and stick to them. Think about what you would be doing if you were working outside your home, and *then do it*. Before you begin your workday, take a half-hour to tidy the kitchen, make the beds, and get rid of clutter. You will find that it is much easier to work when your surroundings are organized.

Deal with friends and neighbors by telling them when you will be available. Just because you are at home does not mean that you are able to drop everything to chat over coffee or on the telephone. You will find that most people respect this. If not, ignore the doorbell and screen your phone calls. Answer business calls and let personal calls go into voice mail, where callers can leave a message. The same goes for the television. Record your favorite soap opera so you can watch it later.

Office Hours or By Appointment Only?

Although home-based businesses are not prone to walk-in traffic, people will tele-phone and expect to reach you during your office hours. If you decide to observe set hours, you must be prepared to stick to them. You are not free to go to the store or take the kids to the park. Unfortunately, you are also unavailable to meet with vendors during the day, when they are open and available. Don't forget that you will have to close completely to accommodate a Saturday wedding.

The best solution is to operate by appointment only, but to be very flexible with the hours in which you conduct these appointments. You will find yourself setting up appointments in the evening and on weekends. If you have an appoint-ment on a Tuesday evening, you can take a block of time for yourself on Tuesday afternoon. This will further enhance your value to the bride and groom.

A Crash Course in Interior Decorating

Decorating your office is similar to decorating other rooms in your home. Be aware of the use of the room and decide on the best furniture arrangement to suit your needs. The color scheme and accessories will round out the look.

Buy only pieces that fit into the overall scheme of the room. Consider durabil-ity, comfort, and quality, but remember that a wedding planner's office must also be beautiful. Analyze the space. Determine whether storage is adequate; you may be able to use closet space elsewhere in the home. It is important to begin with a floor plan drawn to scale on quarter-inch graph paper.

If you apply the basic principles of interior design to your office space, you'll be pleased with the results. Keep in mind, though, that some of the most beauti-fully-decorated rooms are ones in which the rules have been broken.

The **Elements of Design** are scale, balance, line, texture and proportion. These are usually conspicuous only when they are absent.

The term **"scale"** refers to the size of one object compared to the size of another. In decorating, we are concerned with five types of scale:

- scale of the room to the furniture

- scale of each piece of furniture to another

- scale of the accessories to the furniture

- scale of the ornamentation (wood carving or upholstery pattern) to the piece

- scale of each part to the whole

Common sense will guide you away from most scale mistakes. Make sure your accessories are not so large as to impede the use of the furniture. Never place very large furniture into a room that is too small.

"Balance" refers to the visual weight of your furniture arrangements, and can be either symmetrical or asymmetrical. Both are created by means of an imaginary line. In symmetrical balance (also called "formal balance") one side of the imaginary line is a mirror image of the other. In asymmetrical balance (also called "informal balance") each side is different, yet the objects are of the same visual weight, thereby balancing the arrangement. We deal with three types of balance in interior decorating:

- floor plan
- wall grouping
- color

You are probably most familiar with the balance of a wall grouping. However, floor plans must also be balanced to avoid the situation in which one end of the room has all the heaviest furniture. Color is balanced by using it in each area of the room.

"Line" refers to these five:

- straight
- curved
- vertical
- horizontal
- diagonal

The eye follows lines, creating optical illusions. Use a horizontal line to make a room appear wider; this draws the eye from side to side. To make a ceiling appear higher, use vertical lines to draw the eye in an upward direction. Curved lines are more feminine and relaxed. Straight lines are more masculine and stately. Diagonal lines are the most dramatic.

"Proportion" is a term which is often used interchangeably with scale, but they are not the same. The difference between them is best explained by two rectangles, one 2 inches x 4 inches and the other 1 inch x 2 inches. One of these rectangles is twice the size of the other; therefore they are not in scale. They are, however, in proportion to each other, since each has a length that is twice the width. Remember this when you try to place a rectangular desk into a square office.

"**Texture**" can add interest to an otherwise uninspired room. Whether you like the glossy look of polished wood, thick-piled carpet, or crisp chintz, you can use a variety of textures to make your office come to life. Be careful not to use too many textures, as they tend to cancel each other out.

In addition to the basic elements, **color** is an important aspect of your décor. Color can create optical illusions. Dark colors or the warm colors (red, yellow, and orange) make a room appear smaller, while light colors or the cool colors (green, blue, and violet) give the appearance of a larger room. When deciding on colors for your office you can choose your favorite hues, pick a color from something that is already in the room, or, use one of the tried-and-true color schemes.

The best interiors can be ruined by poor **lighting**. Avoid lighting that is too subdued to be adequate. On the other hand, be sure to stay away from harsh and glaring lighting that is too bright. Your desk lamp must provide enough light for your comfort level. In addition, you need lighting in the area in which your clients will sit. Be sure it is adequate for looking at pictures and samples. Be aware of the differences in a color's appearance when it is viewed under fluorescent light as opposed to incandescent. Never purchase fabric or wallpaper without first bringing home a sample and looking at it under various lighting conditions.

It is an insult to your individuality to work in an office that has been designed for someone else. Don't copy every detail from a model room or a magazine picture. Use it for inspiration, but create a room that reflects your own personality.

Office Equipment

Whether you have a home office or rented office space, the equipment you need will be similar. We can divide it into several categories:

FURNITURE AND DÉCOR: Before you shop for your office, you must have an idea of the style and colors in which you wish to decorate. Make a list of the furnishings you want, and measure to be sure everything fits. Consider such items as

- desk
- desk chair
- filing cabinet(s)

- computer desk and chair
- display/storage
- guest chairs
- tables
- lighting
- window coverings
- area rug
- plants

ELECTRONICS: Today's office is more efficient than ever before, thanks to modern technology. Your office might include

- computer
- telephone
- laptop computer
- fax machine
- photocopier
- television/DVD player
- radio

GENERAL EQUIPMENT: Here we have items that do not fit into the other two categories, yet are too permanent to be considered supplies, such as

- brief case
- shredder
- desk accessories
- bulletin board
- appointment book
- safe
- general office equipment (scissors, stapler, etc)

OFFICE SUPPLIES: These are the consumables, and include

- pens and pencils
- letterhead and envelopes
- printer ink
- paper
- staples
- tape
- file folders
- glue
- paper clips

Most cities have large business supply warehouses. Their prices are generally more reasonable than those of smaller stores. As well, consider the possibility of used equipment. Many of these items can be postponed, making them easier to afford; some are optional. For example, a small photocopier is handy, but copies can be easily made at your local print shop. You may not need a desk computer if you already own a laptop. Or, maybe a television wouldn't get any use in your office.

The Business Telephone

You might decide (at least at the beginning) to use your existing telephone line for both personal and business calls. Whether you continue to do so depends on several factors:

- Do you have teenagers?
- Does your husband also use this telephone for his business calls?
- Do you want a business listing in the telephone directory and the Yellow Pages?
- Do your small children frequently answer the phone?

Eventually, you may want a telephone listed under your business name. If the current situation has been working well, simply convert your existing number and continue as before. The monthly bill will be higher, but it's tax deductible. This will entitle you to a business listing in the telephone directory and the Yellow Pages.

If your business calls conflict with those of your teenaged daughter, install a
business line separate from your personal line. The telephone company will have
to rewire your existing system, for a fee. If you don't have a separate answering
machine, subscribe to the phone company's voice mail. Call waiting and call display are must-haves for a business.

Clients are likely to hear your telephone voice before they meet you face-to-
face. Smile when you answer the phone—it will show in your voice! But beware:
phoniness will also show. How does your voice sound over the telephone? Ask
friends and relatives for feedback.

If you have call waiting and voice mail services from the phone company, callers will be able to leave a message if you are out of the office. Do not allow your
children to answer your business line. Never put a caller on hold to answer the
other line. Let calls go into voice mail when you are meeting with a client. Be sure
to return calls promptly; if you wait, you may find that the caller has hired
another wedding planner!

Take your time when composing an outgoing message for your voice mail. Be
sure to include the following:

- Thank the caller
- Identify the business
- Invite the caller to leave a message
- Provide an e-mail address and fax number, if desired
- Invite callers to visit your Web site.

Setting Up Your Filing System

In a well-organized office, you should be able to place your hands on any file
immediately. Although this sounds unrealistic, it is actually easy to achieve.

The legal size allows for wider files, which are very handy in the wedding-planning business. Plan for the storage of "dead files," those you must keep although
you no longer need to access them. Use another area of your home if office space
is limited. Use colorful files to color-code your filing system. Print the labels on
your computer for a tidy and well-organized look. Set up your files with the following headings. Make any changes that will make the filing system uniquely
yours.

Vendors: Have a file for each category, such as caterers, photographers, florists, etc. Keep up-to-date brochures, menus, price lists, and anything else pertaining to these services.

Bookkeeping: All receipts and records of financial transactions go into this file immediately, before they are lost! Every week, enter them into the cash journal and place all receipts in an envelope labeled for the current month. File this envelope in the bookkeeping file. Anything that can be used for your office-at-home expense can be placed in a labeled envelope and saved for your accountant. After tax time, place all receipts and records in a manila envelope labeled with the year, and store in the dead files

Banking: Everything to do with your business account for the current year goes into this file. Store with tax records in the dead files.

Advertising: Include a draft of your brochure, logo, ideas for future ads, and anything else to do with your advertising or your Web site.

Weddings: Keep a separate file for each wedding you are working on. One month after the wedding, move the file to your dead files but do not dispose of it.

Telephone: Include your Yellow Pages contracts.

Legal: Include drafts of your contract, as well as any legal papers obtained from your lawyer.

Inventory: Keep a complete inventory of your business equipment, itemized. Also include notes on depreciation from your accountant.

Subscriptions and Memberships: This file is for all wedding-related publications, associations, and newsletters.

Storage Solutions

Organized storage doesn't just happen. It comes as the result of good planning.

Examine your storage possibilities. They include desk drawers, closed cabinets, open baskets, and display cabinets. If this is inadequate, consider using a spare closet in another area of the house for dedicated storage of business records, extra supplies, and seldom-used objects.

Anything that is kept on open shelves or in cabinets with glass doors must be attractively arranged. That is not to say that everything else can be disorganized and messy! There is a connection between the orderliness of your office and the orderliness of your thoughts. It is difficult to concentrate if your surroundings are not well-arranged. Desk drawers, filing cabinets, and storage closets must be kept tidy.

There are many organizing products available, such as drawer dividers that can keep everything ready to access at a moment's notice. Try to group similar objects together. Any small items that are to be stored in closets or closed cabinets can be placed in labeled boxes. This allows stacking, which will enable you to store more objects in the allotted space.

Make your storage attractive. Shelves of books look better if small decorative objects and plants are interspersed among them. Wicker baskets placed on shelves above eye level can hold small objects, although they will appear to be merely decorative. On the floor, they can hold wedding magazines.

Ambiance

A wedding planner's office has to be as beautiful and elegant as it is efficient. This will show your clients that you have good taste and that you are able to create the kind of atmosphere any bride would want for her wedding.

If you rent decorative items to your clients, they can double as office accessories. Nothing gives an air of elegance more quickly than the stateliness of tall columns or the luster of your silver candelabra!

Quiet music playing in the background is a must! If you feel at all isolated in your one-woman office, play background music continuously.

Offer your clients coffee and tea, served from a silver tea set with your best china. Or, perhaps your clients would prefer a cold drink from your best crystal. A small dish of nuts or mints, or a silver tray of wedding truffles is a nice touch.

On your office walls, amid your certificates, diplomas, and awards, hang framed thank-you notes and pictures of former weddings. This cannot help but increase your image in the eyes of a newly-engaged couple.

If your office has a fireplace, light it when the weather's cold. Other times of the year, set a large arrangement of flowers in the opening. Light several candles and place them throughout the room. If a bride feels good in your office, she is more likely to feel good about hiring you.

Your Professional Library

Keep a library of wedding and business books in your office for quick reference. No matter how much knowledge and experience you have, there will be things you will need to look up. In addition to information books, display a couple of coffee table books. My favorites are *Royal Wedding Dresses* and *Legendary Brides*.

Buy one or two wedding magazines every season. This will allow you to keep up with the changing trends. Keep the latest copy in your office for clients to leaf through if they get stuck for ideas.

A good dictionary and thesaurus are a must for any office. And hopefully *this* book will be a valuable addition to your reference library!

For Your Notes

5

CREATING A WEB SITE

What *is* a Web Site?

Your Web site is your very own home on the World Wide Web. There are literally hundreds of thousands of Web sites dedicated to weddings. A great number of those belong to wedding planners who know that they can double their volume simply by having a presence on the Web. In fact, you may have found out about this book during a visit to the *Sandcastles* Web site.

A Web site is like a twenty-four-hour infomercial about your business, yet it costs a mere fraction of what those half-hour television spots are worth.

A Web site consists of any number of pages. Each page is accessed by clicking on a link on the index page or home page. The pages are written in "Hyper Text Markup Language" or "html," the basics of which you will learn in this chapter. They are then uploaded, or moved from your computer to cyberspace. This is done by using special software called "file transfer protocol." When you want to make changes to your Web site, simply use the word processor of your computer, then upload the page again.

Types of Web Sites

The **Image Web Site** is the most common for wedding planners. It literally establishes your image in the eyes of the potential client. It can be elegant, fun, or anything in between, but it must reflect your business.

The **Store Web Site** is one on which the customer can view merchandise and make purchases using a credit card. It is set up through a third party service and requires much more maintenance than the other types. Many companies sell their products over their Web site.

The **Service Web Site**, as the name implies, offers a service to its visitors. There are many sites that give medical information; these are a perfect example.

The **Relationship Web Site** actually builds a relationship with its visitors. It invites them to come back regularly. Often there is a "blog" on the site (a regularly-updated online journal).

Who Will Design Your Web Site?

Most business owners have their Web sites professionally designed. You will find Web designers in the Yellow Pages. The average site costs over $1,000 to design, but there are alternatives. Contact a local college and hire a student to design your site. Or, do it yourself—I designed my own award-winning Web site using the information I will present to you in this chapter. As well, there are many software applications that will take you step-by-step through the process.

Even if you decide to have someone else design your Web site, be sure to have a hand in its content. An expert in computers is not an expert on weddings. You are the actual designer of the site; the professional is there to help you get the Web site you want. Doesn't that sound like your relationship with the bride?

Once the Web site is designed and uploaded, do not neglect it. We've all seen sites that have never been updated; a visitor immediately wonders if they have gone out of business. Change it, improve it, and keep it evolving, just as your business does.

Hosting Your Web Site

The server you are currently using to provide your Internet service will most likely be able to host your site, as well. You will pay a small monthly fee, in addition to your domain registration. Or, try a hosting company.

You will also encounter companies who will host your Web site free of charge. This may be an option if you are starting out on a shoestring. There are, however, three major drawbacks. First, they are smaller than the big hosting companies, and may be unable to handle your business as it grows. Depending upon the number of hits your Web site receives in a single day, your site may crash, and may even cause the host's site to crash at the same time. You will then be faced with the task of moving to a larger host, just at a time when you are very busy.

The second disadvantage is that they place their sponsors' ads all over your Web pages. That's how they are able to offer their services free to you. It's a trade off, but it cheapens the look of your site. In some cases, they pick keywords from your site to match the ads with related topics to yours. You could end up advertising your competition!

Thirdly, a smaller host is not as helpful to you at a time when you are new to all the technical jargon.

Personal Web Space and Domains

Most Internet service providers include about 60 MG of "personal Web space." You may be unaware you have it. You're paying for it, so why not let your business benefit from it?

This is adequate while you are just starting out, but eventually you will want a higher profile on the Web, which brings us to domain names.

Your host company will assign you an I.P. address. This is a series of numbers separated by dots, such as "http://123.45.67.89." It is definitely not something that would readily identify your business, so most business owners also register a domain name. Domains are registered for one, two, or three years, after which they must be renewed. You may choose your own name or your business name. Incidentally, the "http" stands for "hyper text transfer protocol."

There are no capital letters, and names run together. You can separate your first and last names by using an underscore, but it becomes awkward to say "underscore" as part of the address.

Once you have chosen a domain name, be sure it isn't already in use. Your hosting company can check it for you. Just because there is no Web site at that address, doesn't mean that the domain is not registered. Once you have registered the domain, you own the exclusive rights to it. However, it is possible for two different companies in the same town to register "sandcastles.com" and "sandcastles.net." Obviously, this would be very confusing to potential clients and should be avoided. Some wedding planners prevent the copying of their domain name by registering all the different suffixes, each for a fee. Unless you have a jealous rival, this is probably going a little too far.

After your domain is registered, have it printed on business cards, letterhead, and in every type of advertising you do.

Web Site Content

You control the content of your Web site. Naturally, you will begin by stating who you are and what you do, but the rest is up to you. Here are some ideas to start you thinking:

- guest book

- packages and fees

- contact information

- monthly wedding planning tips

- photos of past weddings (ask permission first)

- FAQ (frequently asked questions)

- blog

- polls

- interactive features

- availability calendar

HTML Basics

Hypertext Markup Language, or html, is used to write the pages that will be uploaded onto your Web site. Even if you will have the site professionally designed, you will need a basic knowledge of html, so you can make minor changes yourself.

Anything that you type will be visible when uploaded unless it is between triangular brackets. These separate the text of the Web page from your instructions which "program" the finished look of the page.

Hyperlinks are used to get from one page to another. Links show up on the finished page as underlined blue text, unless you specify otherwise. After you have clicked on the link, it will show up in red. The html for a hyperlink is

- <a href="page2.html">Page 2</a>

Notice that the instructions are in triangular brackets. The "a href" means that you are creating a link. The "a" is called an "anchor" and "href" stands for "hypertext reference." The slash means that you are cancelling an instruction. Everything not included in brackets will be shown as a blue link. Inside the brackets, "page2" is followed by the suffix "html," which tells the computer to search for a file written in hypertext markup language.

When you scan and save a picture, it will be in "jpg" (joint photographic group) or "gif" (graphic interchange format). To insert a picture onto your Web page, use this html:

- <img width="100"img height="100"img src="picture.jpg">

For a larger picture, increase the values given for the height and width.

- Control the size of the font using <font size>

"1" is normal. To go smaller than normal, use <font size="-1">
To go larger than normal, use <font size="+1">
"-2" and "+2" will give you smaller or larger text respectively. Use </font size> to go back to normal.

- <font face="old english"> lets you specify a font.

Some browsers cannot support fancy fonts, so it is best to stay with Times New Roman, the font you are reading now. To add only one line in a different font, use <font face="old english">line of text</font>

- Use <font color="red"> to change the color of the text. If you do not specify a color, the text will be in black. To revert to black after a color change, use </font color>

- To use a jpg or gif picture as the background of a Web page, give the file a name, and use <background="bkgnd.jpg">

- For a solid color, <background color="light blue">

- <strong> or <b> will give you bold print.

- Use </strong> or </b> to return to normal.

- <li> allows you to list items with bullets.

- </li> returns to normal.

- <p> begins a new paragraph.
 begins a new line.

Organizing Your Web Site

A prospective client's first impression of you is often your Web site; it must be well-organized. Have someone else try to navigate it and report the problems they encounter.

Compare your Web site to a book. The index page is the table of contents, linking to each chapter. Each chapter will link to specific pages of information. Many Web sites have site maps, which are not difficult to create. The site map shows each page in a logical flow.

Make each page consistent, with the same font and text color. Use your logo and company name on each page. Let each page tell about only one subject. You will create confusion if you try to fill a page with unrelated information.

Don't assume that a visitor to your site will know what to do. When you provide a link to another page, tell them "Click here for more information on our packages." Make it easy for a visitor to travel throughout the site by placing links on each page, either at the bottom or down the left-hand side.

Search Engines

Now that you have a great-looking Web site, how will people know you're out there? A limited number will see your Web address on your advertising or business cards. The majority of visitors to your new site will find you through a search engine.

Search engines use keywords to look for Web sites. A potential client will type in a keyword and a "spider" will search the Web for sites containing this word. To increase your chances of being close to the top of the listings, place "meta tags" in the heading of your html. An example of the meta tags used for a wedding-planning business would be

<meta name="keywords"content=wedding, weddings, wedding planner, wedding planning, planning a wedding, consultant, planner, bride, groom>

At the time of this writing, Google is the most popular search engine In fact, "to google" has become a verb, meaning to use a search engine. Of course, you're going to want to google yourself and see how many times your name comes up!

If you search for "weddings" on Google, you will see literally millions of Web sites. It is necessary to narrow down the search. By typing weddings+Paris you will see only sites that pertain to weddings in that particular city.

E-mail

Visitors to your Web site may wish to contact you. Make it easy for them by creating a link to your e-mail. Somewhere on the page, probably close to your address and telephone number, add the following line of html, substituting your e-mail address for mine:

<a href="mailto:sandcastles@sharibeck.com">sandcastles@sharibeck.com</a>

This will show up on your Web page as a link that, when clicked, will open the viewer's e-mail with your address already in the address line. If you are invit-

ing visitors to e-mail you for a specific reason, for example, to request a brochure, you can also fill in the subject line:
<a href="mailto:sandcastles.sharibeck.com?subject=Request_For_a_Brochure"> sandcastles@sharibeck.com</a>

Note that the underscore is used in place of each space.

Banner Ads, Links to Other Web Sites, and Web Rings

Banners are wide, rectangular ads that will link you to another Web site. Many business owners exchange banners. They increase the amount of traffic to your Web site, but they tend to cheapen its appearance. Remember that wedding planners must do everything in the best of taste. Chances are the visitor won't be back.

Occasionally, a site with a directory of wedding-related businesses will place your name and link on their site in exchange for a banner on yours. This is the one time I do approve of banners, as this will identify you as a member of the wedding-planning community. Even then, place them all together on a separate Web page named "Links."

Your Web site's ranking in the search engines depends upon how many other sites are linked to yours. This is a good way to attract additional traffic, but you must be careful to link only to other wedding-related sites. Again, these should be on a separate "Links" page.

When you join a Web ring, you place your Web site in a group of others with the same purpose. Limit your participation to only one ring to avoid adding clutter to your site.

Spelling

It is imperative that you carefully check the spelling on your Web site. Nothing will destroy your credibility faster than an amateur site full of errors.

Note that the "W" in "Web site" is capitalized, as are all the words in "World Wide Web," and the "I" in Internet.

Many wedding planners misspell words that they use as part of their daily work, and it is important not to confuse their spelling with that of their homonyms.

- Bridal means "pertaining to the bride." A bridle is a head harness for a horse.

- Stationery is a word for wedding invitations and other related items. Stationary means "to be fixed in one place."

- An altar is the raised area at the front of the church before which the bride and groom stand. To alter something is to change it.

For Your Notes

6

RUNNING AN EFFICIENT BUSINESS

Time Management

To manage your time well, you must be both efficient and effective. Effective people are not necessarily efficient, but efficient people are effective. They know how to do the right job the right way. Time management experts tell us that there are fixed techniques to improve efficiency.

- Create a routine for tasks that are performed regularly. This frees your mind to schedule the other tasks.

- Consolidate tasks that can be done at the same time. If you have an appointment with a photographer, you may be able to mail a contract while you're out of the office.

- Delegate jobs to others who can handle them better than you. You may not have realized it, but every time you hire a vendor, you are doing just that.

- Reorganize your environment to make it easier for you to handle the various tasks that make up your day. Be sure your office is well-equipped. Always put things back where they belong.

- Plan ahead. Organize each day's schedule the night before. Pull a client's file before they arrive for the meeting.

- Simplify if possible. Consider alternatives. Do you *really* need to set up a meeting with your client, or is it something you can handle over the phone?

Always stick to only one calendar. Many business people use two—one for business and one for their personal lives. Keeping one calendar will eliminate the possibility of scheduling conflicts. If your daughter's dance recital is at 7:30, you can't possibly make an 8:00 meeting with a caterer across town. Don't schedule too tightly; it's best to leave some breathing room.

Setting Your Priorities

Many wedding planners have trouble finishing the jobs that must be done each day, either because they cannot prioritize, or because they are distracted by less important tasks.

In the 1930's, when Charles Schwab was in charge of Bethlehem Steel, he hired expert Ivy Lee to help him with this very problem. Lee came up with the following plan, and told Schwab to send him a check for whatever he thought it was worth. Schwab paid him $25,000 for his idea, a great deal of money today, but even more back then! It has since been printed in many organizing books and has been the topic of many seminars. Here's the valuable advice:

- Make a list of everything that must be done tomorrow. Do it tonight so you are not too rushed in the morning. Number each item on the list according to importance. Tomorrow, do the number one task first, and then number 2, and so on, down the list. Don't worry about finishing everything, because the most important jobs will be complete. Anything left over can be transferred to the next day's list.

It feels good to have the jobs of lesser importance on paper and not nagging in your mind. You don't have to worry about whether a low-priority job is a nine or a ten. Just place a number beside it. If it gets postponed onto three or more lists, maybe you can eliminate it. Don't write more than ten tasks on your list at one time, as it can be overwhelming.

Analyzing Your Use of Time

If you work hard all day and still have no time to finish, analyze how your time is actually being spent.

Set up a sheet of paper with seven days in half-hour increments. Throughout the day, note how you are spending your time. Don't record what you *should* have been doing, only what you have actually done. At the end of each day, your page should be filled with items such as these:

- telephone (personal)

- telephone (business)
- meetings (business)
- shopping
- banking
- children
- husband
- reading (personal)
- reading (business)
- watching TV
- paperwork (personal)
- paperwork (business)
- eating
- sleeping
- personal care

After the first week, highlight the times in which you did what you had planned to do. Analyze what went wrong during the other times.

You may have planned a task for a time when it was not possible to carry it out efficiently. You cannot do your filing and spend quality time with your children simultaneously. If you schedule your filing for a time when your family needs you, you will not be working at your best. If you plan to do your banking during peak hours, you will be spending more time than necessary standing in line.

You may be ignoring your body's natural rhythms. If you are at your best in the morning, schedule your demanding tasks early. On the other hand, give yourself a chance to wake up slowly if you are a night person.

You may be allowing too many interruptions. Don't answer the door or the phone, and keep the television turned off.

You may not be able to focus on a task if you do not have clearly-defined goals. Or, perhaps the task is irrelevant and can be delegated or deleted.

You may need to arrange your schedule so that you do not need to repeat steps. Go to the bank on the way to an appointment instead of travelling the same route twice.

You may not have the necessities to complete the job. If you have to run out for file folders in the middle of reorganizing the office, you will not get the job done.

You may be procrastinating. Read on …

Solving the Procrastination Problem

Procrastination is a form of self-sabotage. Most people do it occasionally, many do it regularly, and some are completely overtaken by it. The first step to solving the procrastination problem is to identify its causes:

- The task is boring or unpleasant
- The task is difficult or overwhelming
- You don't know where to start
- There's no real thanks for it
- You are worried that you may not do a good job

Some people procrastinate because the job is boring and they like the adrenalin rush they experience when they have to work against a deadline. It may be possible to delegate the job, or perhaps a false deadline will work. Move up your deadline by promising to have your books to the accountant by an earlier date. You will feel the adrenalin rush sooner and be done ahead of schedule.

If the task is too difficult, you may be able to ask for help. If you accept the job of decorating a reception hall you will not be able to do the work yourself. It involves at *least* two people, preferably more, to hang tulle swags from a ceiling. If you commit to doing the work alone you are very likely to procrastinate. Perhaps you have taken on a task you have never been trained to do. Now is the time to learn! Overwhelming jobs are best broken down into manageable chunks. The completion of each is an accomplishment in itself. By successfully finishing one, you will be motivated to continue to the next. Before you know it, you'll be finished! Break down the job into smaller time increments. When compiling your daily to-do list, try to identify jobs that you find difficult. If you find yourself uneasy or suddenly tense, this may be one of those tasks. Anything you dread doing (unless it can be delegated or eliminated) should be done first. That way, it's over more quickly and you won't be dreading it while trying to get through your other jobs.

If you are not sure where to begin, sit down for fifteen minutes and think about the job. What would be the logical starting point? Can you just jump in anywhere? What is the end result? After fifteen minutes get up and begin, even if you have to start in the middle and work your way out.

If the job has no thanks or reward, create one of your own. Buy a book or a DVD that you've been wanting for awhile. Set it on your desk and let it be the reward for finishing the job—no cheating allowed!

If you don't think you will do a good job, you will probably procrastinate. Break the job into smaller tasks and examine each one. Are there skills involved that you don't have? Ask for help, delegate, or learn quickly. Think of it as a way to increase your knowledge and ability. The next time a similar job comes along you'll be ready!

Make Use of Small Blocks of Time

It's amazing what you can accomplish in five, ten, or fifteen minutes! Throughout the day, we find ourselves with small blocks of time that can be used to accomplish many small tasks.

FIVE MINUTES:

- Check your e-mail
- Check your voice mail
- Put something away
- Do a quick tidy-up of your desk top
- Address a letter
- Send a fax
- Send an e-mail
- Tidy a desk drawer

TEN MINUTES:

- File a stack of papers
- Proofread
- Return a telephone call
- Weed out a file

- Bank online or by telephone
- Clean out your briefcase

FIFTEEN MINUTES:

- Update your Web site
- Begin an article
- Plan a menu
- Reconcile your bank account
- Begin to think about your new advertising strategies

Setting Goals

If you don't know where you're going, you'll never know if you're there. Setting goals will let you see where your business is going. You might have one main goal or several smaller ones. Some will be long-term, others immediate. Some will be concrete, others abstract. But how do you know if you have a goal you can reach? Let's start with an example, a goal common to all wedding planners:

My goal is for my business to be successful.

This is a sincere goal, but one that can never be reached because it is not specific. How are we to measure success?

My goal is for my business to make lots of money.

Make your goals as specific as possible. In this case there is a criterion. "Success" means financial success. But we must find out what this wedding planner means by "lots of money."

My goal is for my business to make enough money for me to live comfortably.

This is impossible to measure. The goal must be more specific.

My goal is for my business to make $5,000 per month. I plan to reach this goal in six months. Within the next five years, I will be making a monthly salary of $10,000. In the meantime, I plan to be making $3,000 per month, starting next month.

This goal is finally specific. However, it is not realistic. Businesses need time to get off the ground. A goal of an immediate salary of $3,000 will never be reached. By rewording with a reasonable dollar figure, the wedding planner will have a goal she can work toward. Remember, goals must be specific, reasonable, and measureable.

Set immediate goals (one week to one month), short-term goals (within six months), and long-term goals (one year or longer). Assign a deadline so that you will know when to assess your goal. Goals are not written in stone; they can be revised at any time.

Business Communication

In today's technological world, we have more methods of business communication than ever before. We have e-mail, voice mail, fax, telephone, cell phone, text messaging, and the written word.

E-mail, short for electronic mail, is sometimes preferable to other forms of communication. It's short, to the point, and flexible. Most importantly, it reaches its destination right away. You can e-mail around the world with no long-distance charges. I once planned a wedding for a bride who lived in another part of the country without meeting her until the evening of the rehearsal! The only drawback? Check your spelling and grammar—once you click "send" you can't get it back!

Your clients are more likely to reach you by voice mail than in person. Your outgoing message should be pleasant and professional. Get a reputation for returning your calls promptly.

Faxes are a convenient form of communication. They can be used for proofing business forms and wedding invitations, sending ideas and sketches to vendors, and ordering from suppliers. If you don't fax often, have the telephone company provide you with a feature called "Ident-a-Call." Two short rings will alert you that a fax is coming in. This way, you can avoid the expense of a dedicated fax line.

Receiving faxes can be expensive, as paper and print film are being consumed. Many businesses once used cover sheets for everything, but they no longer add another sheet of paper. However, there will be times when they are necessary. If you need to send a fax to a bride at her place of work, a cover sheet will allow your faxes to find their way to her desk.

Cell phones and text messaging were tailor-made for wedding planners. It is especially important for vendors to reach you when you are on-site the day of a wedding, and cell phones make this easy.

All of these new toys cannot replace the written letter, note, or memo. When writing, be considerate of the reader. Keep to the point and be as brief as possible. Most experts recommend three paragraphs at the most. Always use your computer's spell-check feature. Even if you are a good speller, it will pick up typing errors. If you are unsure as to the proper form for a business letter, invest in an up-to-date book on business etiquette.

Using Your Computer to Get Organized

Much of the information on your computer can be stored on disc in a much smaller space than hard copy (paper copies) would take. Each disc can hold a large amount of information, separated into files. Be sure to review the discs regularly and delete obsolete information. Anything entered into the computer must be saved to disc. If you have ever lost data due to a computer malfunction you know how important this step can be.

To keep vendors' information in one place and within easy reach, start a disc on which the vendors are arranged in folders.

Put your address book on disc. You can update the disc whenever a contact changes their address or telephone number.

Hand-held and palm computers have built-in organizing programs. For PCs, these programs can be purchased and installed at a reasonable cost. They can be used to organize just about every aspect of your wedding-planning business, including finances. Daily planners display increments of hours, half-hours, or quarter-hours. Calendars display the day, week, month, or quarter. Visual prompts remind you of deadlines.

Save paper by putting your to-do list on the computer. Simply delete the task when it is completed.

Use your computer to design your own wedding-planning program. Keep each wedding on a separate disc. Use the following directions.

Creating Your Own Wedding-Planning Computer Program

There is a great deal of wedding-planning software on the market; perhaps you have even downloaded a demo version. The graphics are beautiful, and they are no doubt useful for a bride and groom planning their own wedding. I never found one to suit my needs, not even the "professional" editions that allow you to track several weddings at a time. I developed my own program, one that I could tailor to suit my own system.

Before you begin, decide what you really need to include. This is the reason you are custom-designing the program. Include only the items you will actually use. To start you thinking, here are some possibilities. Feel free to use or adapt the ideas as you see fit.

Folder entitled "Planning Info"

- Date and location of wedding
- The Bride: All information pertinent to the bride, such as name, address, home and business telephone numbers, e-mail; parents' names and telephone numbers
- The Groom: All information pertinent to the groom, such as name, address, home and business telephone numbers, e-mail; parents' names and telephone numbers
- Preferences: Type of wedding, degree of formality, color scheme
- The Wedding Party: For each member of the wedding party, information such as name, address, home and business telephone numbers, e-mail

Folder entitled "The Ceremony"

- The Church: All pertinent information including name of church, address, telephone and fax numbers; directions; clergy's name and telephone number; notes on parking facilities, wheelchair access, decorations, restrictions
- The Ceremony: Special readings; Scripture; will the couple write their own vows?
- The Music: All selections for the prelude music, processional, ceremony, and recessional; the name and telephone numbers of the organist and soloist
- Checklists: All details pertaining to the above; all tasks to be completed

Folder entitled "The Guests"

- Logistics: Number of guests; children; wheelchairs; other special considerations. You are not concerned with the actual guest list, so leave that to the bride and groom.
- The Invitations: Printer's name, address, telephone and fax numbers; number of invitations; paper style, ink colors, font styles, etc; other stationery items.

Folder entitled "The Reception"

- The Venue: List possible locations, to be replaced by the final choice. For each location include all pertinent information such as name of venue, address, telephone and fax numbers, e-mail; Web site; contact person; directions.

- The Caterer: Name, address, telephone and fax numbers; contact person; payment and due dates; menus

- The Wedding Cake: Baker's name, address, telephone and fax numbers; description of cake, flavors, icing; payment and due dates

Folder entitled "Vendors"

- The Florist: Name, address, telephone and fax numbers; personal flowers, including cost and description; ceremony and reception flowers, including cost and description; other items; payments and due dates.

- DJ/Musicians: Contact person's name, telephone number; information on each band member; costs, deposit due dates; specific songs

- Rentals: For each rental location name, address, telephone and fax numbers; items needed; description and costs; deposit and payment information

- Photographer: name address, telephone and fax numbers; package information and all costs; back-up information; list of required shots

- Videographer: name address, telephone and fax numbers; package information and all costs; back-up information; list of required shots

- Transportation: Name, address, telephone and fax numbers; contact person; type of vehicle; directions; driver's cell number

Folder entitled "Formal Wear"

- A different page for each member of the wedding party with such information as name, address, telephone number; store location; contact person; sizes; style numbers, descriptions, prices; fittings and alteration schedules

Folder entitled "Timeline"

- One page, for each of the months preceding the wedding; all time-related information, vendor payments

- One page for each of the two weeks prior to the wedding; all time-related information, vendor payments

- One page for the wedding day schedule

Folder entitled "Thoughts and Inspirations"

- Use this one as you see fit

The instructions for creating your own program are quite simple, using the word processor software on your computer.

1. Create a new folder

2. Name the folder

3. Open the folder, and select font size and style

4. Begin entering information

5. When done, close the page and save the changes

6. Repeat these steps to set up remaining folders

7. Save to disc

8. Label the disc with the names of the bride and groom and the wedding date

If your computer or software allows, you can add scanned photographs to your program, customizing it even further.

As an alternative, you may wish to use your computer's spreadsheet software. The program supplies you with "cells," upon which you can organize your information with little or no effort. You can also create boxes of any size in which to type text that does not belong in any of the cells.

The first page will be "Planning Info." The cells on the page can be customized by changing the fonts and colors, and will be labeled as follows:

- Leave cell A:1 blank

- Label B:1, C:1, etc. with the titles Bride, Groom, Best Man, Maid of Honor, etc.

- Label cells A:2, A:3, A:4, etc. with the titles Name, Address, Home Telephone, etc.

The information can now be inserted into the boxes. Add a text box to record preferences. Use this to record such ideas as degree of formality, style, etc. Finally, save the spreadsheet to disc, and label the disc with the couple's names and the wedding date.

"The Ceremony"

This will be set up as the Planning Info page, so that you can enter the name and address of the church, and the names and telephone numbers of the clergy, organist, and soloist. In a text box, record details such as parking and wheelchair accessibility. In a second text box, note any special vows or readings that will be part of the ceremony. In a third text box, record the chosen music for the prelude, processional, ceremony, and recessional.

At this time, begin a to-do list on a separate page. Label the row of cells with the task, the person responsible for the task, the date it is to be done, and the date it is finalized. Refer back to this sheet as you fill out the others. In the meantime, add the tasks the must be done in conjunction to the ceremony.

"The Guests"

Although the guest list itself is not one of your concerns, you must keep track of the numbers. Note the number of children, special needs, or allergies. Use a text box to record the date the invitations are to be ordered (and from whom), as well as the date they must be mailed. Add these to your to-do list. Also note font, ink color, paper, etc.

"The Reception"

Open a separate sheet for the venue, wedding cake, caterer, and other vendors. Again, label the rows and columns so that you can record names, telephone numbers, fax numbers, etc. Include cells for payment due dates and amounts. Use text boxes for such information as directions, menus, etc.

"Vendors"

Open a separate sheet for each vendor, or place them all on the same sheet so that it resembles the Planning Info sheet. This will be determined by the amount of information you must enter, and the size and quantities of the text boxes you will need.

"Formal Wear"

It is best to use two sheets, one for the ladies and one for the men. Set up both the same way as the Planning Info sheet. Change the labels to include dress/suit sizes, shoe sizes, measurements, manufacturer/style numbers, fitting schedules, and payments.

"Thoughts and Inspirations"

This page will consist of many text boxes, and it will be one you will return to often.

"Monthly Calendars"

Label each sheet with the months until the wedding, counting backwards. Label the cells according to the day and the tasks that must be done that day. This can be set up horizontally, or you can adjust the cells to make them look like the squares of a calendar. Transfer all items from your to-do list.

"Time Lines"

Create a time line of the week before the wedding and another of the wedding day. Follow the instructions in the following section.

Computerized Time Lines

Using your computer's spreadsheet program, organize the week before the wedding, as well as the wedding day itself.

The first time line will allow you to track the many details in the week leading up to the wedding. Open a sheet which you will name "Week of _____." Leave cell A:1 blank. Label cells B:1, C:1, D:1, etc with the days of the week, ending with the day before the wedding. Assuming the wedding is on a Saturday, the days will be labeled from Sunday to Friday. Cells A:2, A:3, A:4, etc., will be labeled from 8:00 AM to 11:00 PM, in half-hour increments.

On the sheet entitled "Wedding Day," map out your entire day, using fifteen-minute increments, starting at 6:00 AM and ending at 2:00 AM the following morning.

Both time lines are used in the same manner. Simply click the cell beside the appropriate time and type in the information.

When you've finished creating the time lines, transfer them to disc. If you are planning to bring your laptop computer to the wedding you will have the time-line at your fingertips. Otherwise, print it out in duplicate the night before.

An Alternative to the Computer Program

Many wedding planners get a great deal of use from their programs. They carry their laptops to every meeting and especially to every wedding. Some planners prefer not to carry a computer or have not yet invested in one; for them we have an alternative. It's how wedding planners worked before computers. It's a notebook, but one of a different kind!

Using a three-ring binder, you will be able to create a complete picture of the wedding. Every detail will be there, ready for you to access it. Use tabulated dividers to separate the sections. Label in a manner similar to the section of the computer program: Planning Info, Ceremony, Reception, etc.

Create pages similar to those of the computer program and insert them into the appropriate section. Most wedding planners punch holes into manila envelopes and use them for holding smaller pieces of paper such as receipts.

I recommend a separate binder for each wedding; some wedding planners like to keep all current weddings together in one binder.

Paper, Paper, Paper!

All businesses seem to create endless amount of paper. There have been countless books written on the subject of eliminating and organizing the paper problem.

Every piece of paper gives you three options:

1. act on it

2. recycle it

3. file it

It is sometimes overwhelming to look at bulging files of paper on the desk. You don't know where to begin. Just remember, it didn't appear overnight, and it's not going to disappear overnight. There are two ways to guarantee a solution:

1. do a little each day

2. handle all new paper the correct way in the meantime

Assemble the following supplies: wastebasket, shredder, accordion file labeled with the months of the year, and file folders labeled according to "Setting up Your Filing System" in Chapter 4. Set a time that is realistic for you, perhaps one hour. During this hour you will target a specific area, such as your desk. The rule is this: handle each piece of paper only once.

As you pick up the paper for the first and only time, decide whether to act on it, file it, or throw it away. "File it" does not mean "file it away until later because you don't know what to do with it." That is a sign that the paper needs to be acted upon, so file it in the accordion file under the appropriate month.

Much of the paper in your office can be recycled. Experts tell us that we only use twenty percent of the paper we store. Papers containing personal information should be shredded for your security.

In order to keep your system working, treat each piece of incoming mail this way. Go through your accordion file at the beginning of every month and add each item to your calendar. When the task is completed, file the paper or recycle it. Be sure to go through your files every six months and recycle anything you no longer need.

Another way to control paper is to get rid of those little scraps with telephone messages on them, and log your calls. You'll read more about logging later in this chapter.

Eliminating Clutter

We are surrounded daily by five different types of clutter. All of them can affect your ability to think clearly, find what you need, and run your wedding-planning business efficiently.

PHYSICAL CLUTTER

This is the best-known clutter, because it involves physical objects. In some cases it can become overwhelming. To solve the problem, you must sell, throw out, or give away all objects that are no longer needed or wanted. Everything left over must be assigned its own space, and must be returned to that space when not in use.

PAPER CLUTTER

We have already discussed paper clutter. If you don't stay on top of the situation, it will return. Never allow a piece of paper that comes into your office to escape your scrutiny. Keep only the paper you need, and weed out your files twice a year to get rid of the excess.

VIRTUAL CLUTTER

E-mail and voice mail have solved some our clutter problems but they have created others. Some people have to shift through many saved messages every week, facing the major task of deciding which can be deleted and which will be saved until next time. Hopefully, they will never have to locate one of their messages!

Voice mail messages should be recorded in your telephone log and deleted. E-mail can be located to one of three created files: action, delegate, and save. The action e-mails can be deleted after they have been acted upon. The delegated e-mails can be forwarded. Saved e-mails can be filed in topic-appropriate files, which are checked regularly to clear out deadwood.

MENTAL CLUTTER

Mental clutter cannot be seen but it is a very real problem. It refers to the many things we carry around that we should just let go of. These include grudges, worries, and overloaded schedules. If left uncontrolled, it can make you physically ill.

The best solution for mental clutter is an organized master list of all the tasks you must complete. Once they are on paper or in your organizer, forget about them. Every evening, prepare a to-do list for the next day, using items from your master list.

On another list, itemize your worries and analyze each one: What are you worried about? What can you do to help? What is the worst that can happen? What can you do then? This exercise will show you just how foolish it is to carry worries around with you. What you are worried about may not even happen, and if it does you can deal with the situation then. In the meantime, count your blessings.

FINANCIAL CLUTTER

Financial clutter is the mishandling of your finances. An account at every bank in town, too many credit cards, and not reconciling your bank account are examples of financial clutter. Consolidate all of your accounts into one savings account and one checking account. The savings account can be an escrow to hold monthly installments toward the payments that you make quarterly, biannually or annually. The checking account will be for your monthly expenses.

You should keep six month's living expenses handy for emergencies, but a savings account does not pay enough interest to make this practical. Instead, put the money into a GIC.

Keeping Documents

Some of your business papers must be kept indefinitely; others may be disposed of after a certain period of time. For the sake of your organized work space, do not store anything that is not necessary. Use this list to decide what you can weed out of your files.

CORRESPONDENCE:

- General—1 year
- Clients—1 year

- Vendors—1 year
- Purchases—1 year
- Legal—indefinitely

ACCOUNTING:

- Cash books—indefinitely
- Bank statements—3 years
- Cancelled checks—7 years
- Deposit slips—3 years
- Ledgers and journals—indefinitely
- Inventory—7 years
- Bank reconciliation—1 year
- Depreciation—indefinitely
- Auditors' reports—indefinitely
- Financial statements—indefinitely
- Record of vendor payments—7 years
- Tax returns—7 years (some experts recommend you keep them indefinitely)

INSURANCE:

- Expired policies—4 years
- Claims, after settlement—7 years
- Fire inspection reports—6 years
- Accident reports—5 years

CORPORATE:

- Charter—indefinitely
- Minute books—indefinitely
- By-laws—indefinitely
- Expired leases and motgages—indefinitely

- Tax returns—indefinitely
- Retirement/pension—indefinitely
- Copyright/trademarks—indefinitely

OTHER BUSINESS PAPERS:

- Employment applications—3 years
- Purchase orders—3 years
- Invoices—3 years
- Personnel contracts, expired—6 years

Logging Telephone Calls

If you use your personal telephone for business, log your calls to determine which percentage can be claimed as a business expense. Even if you have a business phone and will be claiming the entire bill, a telephone log is a handy way to keep track of the calls you have made to your clients.

A telephone log can also solve a disagreement. If a client tells you that you never returned her call, you can pinpoint the date and time when you did in fact speak to her. Keep a notebook beside the phone, and record in it the following information:

- Date of call
- Time
- Incoming or outgoing
- Name of party
- Telephone number
- Length of call
- Reason for call
- Action required
- Action taken (with date)

If the client is away from the telephone, record in your log that you left a message. As well, log messages that have been left for you; in this case, the action required is to return the call.

The Reality Check

Each year, perhaps on the anniversary of starting your business, perform a reality check. First, list everything that you did during the past year to help grow your business. Simply brainstorm the ideas; they need not be in any particular order. Leave a small space beside each.

Next, jot down beside each item the results you saw. Be as specific as you can. For example:

"Wedding Wonderland" ad in Daily Star, December 20XX: ten inquiries, one wedding booked.

Next, analyze each result. Was the action successful in building new business? Sometimes, you can be very busy and still be unproductive. Unless you take the time to conduct a reality check, you may confuse activity with action. If you have found a successful item, add it to your plans for the next year. If it wasn't successful, perhaps it can be changed for the better. Otherwise, don't repeat it.

Finally, review your goals from last year. How many did you reach? Are they still relevant? Put your new set of goals in writing, and bring them out this time next year for another reality check.

For Your Notes

7

PROMOTING YOUR BUSINESS

Marketing Basics

"Marketing" is a business term for the system that determines how goods and services are passed between the source and the consumer (or between the wedding planner and the bride). To market your wedding-planning business you must use a combination of advertising, publicity, and public relations.

The first step in marketing is pricing your service. We covered this topic in Chapter 2; review it if you wish. For now, be aware of the psychology of pricing. Most people pay more attention to the first number in a price, and trick themselves into seeing $1,999 as much lower than $2,000. Most retail stores and service businesses take advantage of this fact.

Leader pricing may work for you. Have a "loss leader" that you give to each couple, such as a free hour of consultation or a free non-alcoholic punch at the reception. You are giving the clients something upon which they can place a dollar figure. In turn, you will receive business from them that you may not have had otherwise.

Don't forget the reason the bride has hired you in the first place. She has a psychological need to have a carefree wedding with quality and prestige. She is actually *less* likely to hire you if you offer bargain-basement pricing. Remember the old saying, "You get what you pay for." Don't price yourself out of the market, but do give your services the value they deserve. Include all extras, such as postage, in your fee. The bride won't feel carefree if you bog her down with all the little details of your business.

Promotion is a variable factor. Simply put, it is how you affect the buying habits of your brides by communicating information about your services. Working with a bride and groom is known as "personal selling." "Mass selling" involves communicating with large groups of potential clients at once. This includes advertising and publicity, as well as handing out promotional items at bridal shows.

Marketing also involves product determination. Decide on the scope of your services. Will you offer full-service wedding planning, or will you handle only certain aspects of the planning process? Will you coordinate theme weddings as a specialty? Will you sell wedding-related products? What type of products? Where will you display these items? Will you rent them out to clients? This brings us to distribution. How will you deliver the seven-foot columns that you plan to rent? Will you send them by courier or hire someone with a truck?

To have a successful business, you must take the proactive approach to marketing. Although planning weddings is what you do best, your most important job is marketing your wedding-planning services. The passive approach is very easy: you run an ad to let everyone know you're open for business, and then you sit back and wait for the world to beat a path to your door. Easy, but ineffective. Proactive marketing involves spending up to fifty percent of your working time attracting clients.

Keep records of each type of promoting you do and how many clients you get from each.

Advertising

Before putting together any sort of advertising campaign, you must examine your target market. In our business, it's quite simple: newly engaged couples, couples in the midst of their wedding planning, couples renewing their wedding vows, and couples marrying for a second time.

Your advertising is more likely to be successful if you plan for the entire year at once. This way, you can take advantage of the built-in timetable that every bride follows.

Anywhere from eight to twelve months before the wedding, the bride is newly engaged and has no idea where to start. From six to eight months before the wedding, if she hasn't already hired a wedding planner, she will have made some plans on her own. This is the point where she will realize that it isn't as easy as it looks. Three months before the wedding, panic is setting in, as the bride realizes that time is running out. If you are able to reach her in any of these stages, you will have a successful advertising campaign.

At the time of this writing, June is still the peak wedding month, with July and August tied for second. Spring and fall are popular among those wishing to avoid the extreme heat. Although the winter months are somewhat quieter, you'll find that the weeks close to Christmas and Valentines Day are in high demand.

In early January, and again in mid-February, try to reach the potential clients who got engaged at Christmas and Valentine's Day. The first three months of the year are for your "Romance" ads. June is the perfect time to reach brides who will be marrying *next* June. This is where you will emphasize "Service." In late August, you will target those who are getting married soon (September and October are popular wedding months). You will be selling your ability to relieve some of the bride's stress by taking much of the weight off her shoulders.

Each bride is important to you. The first will use your complete wedding-planning package. The second will use some of your services, and the third will want you at the wedding and reception to implement her plans.

Work out your advertising budget ahead of time. Money spent now in advertising will pay off later. Eventually, you will find that your ads will more than pay for themselves.

Don't consider "transit advertising," the kind you see on the side of a bus or in a bus shelter. It is not at all suited to the professional image you wish to project. Business people in all walks of life give away pens and key rings with advertising on them. It can become costly and reaches a limited audience, but as long as you keep it tasteful and high-end, try it if you like.

PRINT ADVERTISING:

Newspaper advertising will probably take up most of your campaign. As a rule, newspapers charge according to the size of the ad and the number of insertions. Ads are sold by "column inches," meaning a certain number of columns wide by a certain number of inches high. Take advantage of multiple insertions—the average person does not respond to an ad the first time they see it. The larger the circulation, the more the ad will cost. If you live in a small town, you may wish to place an ad in the newspaper of the nearest city. When you have decided on the size of the ad, you are ready to design it. Be careful to target only one aspect of your business so that you do not confuse the reader. Have the ad placed in the lifestyle section, or better yet, find out when they will be publishing a wedding feature.

Design the ad on your computer and provide the newspaper with "camera ready" work. Clip art, small drawings provided by a printer, can be used. Be aware that using someone else's clip art is against copyright laws.

Make your ads recognizable. Use your logo every time. A border will make it stand out, and be sure to leave plenty of "white space." Avoid "I" and "we." Instead of, "I will make all your wedding dreams come true," say, "All your wedding dreams will come true." Don't fall into the trap of decorating your ad with tacky little hearts and wedding bells.

If you have a business telephone, the best place to advertise is in the Yellow Pages. This is where brides look when they are ready to buy. When I featured my business in the Yellow Pages, I had my one-line listing in the town in which I live but I ran my larger ad in Toronto instead.

It is helpful to advertise on Internet wedding directories, even if you haven't yet designed your Web site. Many are free of charge; others charge a nominal fee.

The bridal magazines are among the thickest on the newsstand. They are also the only magazines in which we actually *want* to see so many ads! They are published semi-annually, which means that each issue is on display for six months. Most have a classified directory toward the back of each issue, containing word ads or business-card ads of small businesses, including wedding planners. These ads are more reasonably priced, so you will recover your costs with the first wedding you book. The full, half, or quarter-page ads are very expensive. Advertising costs vary from publication to publication, so call the ones you're interested in for prices. Generally, they will give you a discount if you place your ad in two or more consecutive issues.

RADIO AND TELEVISION:

Radio and television are two media that rarely feature advertising from wedding planners. That is not to say that you cannot venture in if you wish.

There are many different kinds of radio stations. The formats run the gamut from all-news stations to those that play the latest dance music. This is where your knowledge of your target audience comes in. You must know the format to choose and the time of day in which to air. There are two ways to advertise on the radio. You can produce a commercial, or you can provide the copy for the DJ, who will simply read it on the air. The latter is less expensive. Radio commercials tend to sound very cliché unless they are professionally-written. Avoid coming across like a used-car salesman, and skip the impulse to write a catchy little jingle. Tasteful classical music in the background, together with a promise of a stress-free wedding day should suffice. Several voices keep the commercial from sounding monotonous. Remember, less is more. Be sure to get a copy of your commercial—you paid for it!

Television commercials can have the same pitfalls as those on the radio. You can instantly spot the amateur attempts; again, keep it simple. Television is an expensive way to advertise, with spots in prime time priced highest. The cost of hiring a producer is prohibitive for a small business. Cable and community television stations are less costly, so start there.

Publicity and Public Relations

Publicity is media exposure that you do not control. Someone submits a story that they wrote about you, or a reporter reports on something you said or did. Publicity is free, and it tends to be believed more than advertising.

Publicity can take many forms. The most common is a simple newspaper story in which you appear. Maybe a local celebrity is getting married and a reporter asks you the details of the wedding plans. I once did an interview for the National Post on the anniversary of September 11; the reporter wanted to know if brides were superstitious about the date.

Perhaps you will be participating in a bridal show. A news release may be sent to the papers and the Internet, and you will benefit from the exposure.

Become active in your community. Although we should help those less fortunate without thought of personal gain, it can't help but increase the public's regard for you if they read that "Mary Smith, a local wedding planner and business woman, volunteers at the local food bank on a weekly basis."

Take on a cause. I began Operation L.overs. L.overs is short for "leftovers." Clients pay a high price for the meal they serve at their wedding reception, and so much food goes to waste. Due to regulations regarding the donation of leftover food to shelters, many leftovers are thrown in the garbage. Through Operation L.overs, I was able to distribute them to the homeless.

Networking

Never miss an opportunity to sell yourself and your business to others. You never know who is getting married, or who knows someone who is. Most areas have networking groups; join as many as you have time for and go to their networking meetings. Collect business cards from everyone you meet, and hand yours out. Volunteer to speak on the subject of weddings at one of their meetings.

Develop your ability to remember names. Say the name of the person with whom you are speaking several times during the conversation. Make eye contact. If you are uncomfortable making eye contact when speaking to someone, look at their nose—they'll never notice the difference. Listen to what the other person is saying, and repeat it in your own words. Don't monopolize the conversation. When introduced to someone, extend your hand immediately.

Network with vendors. Many of them will be members of the Board of Trade, Chamber of Commerce, or Women in Business groups. Get to know them personally. Be genuinely interested. Develop a rapport. Vendors can be your best allies, and definitely your best source of referrals.

Bridal shows are a great opportunity to network directly with brides. We will cover everything you need to know about bridal shows in Chapters 8 and 9.

It is important that you network with the right people. You will meet four personality types at the average meeting:

- The Know-It-All: She is aggressive, offering unwanted advice to anyone in the room.

- The Shy Girl: She may be new to the group. She will pretend to be busy so that she can avoid talking to anyone.

- The User: She will call you only when she needs a favor, and she will never reciprocate.

- The Professional: She exchanges ideas and advice and helps the Shy Girl. Build a quality relationship with her.

As in any social situation, networking has its own set of rules and etiquette. Use the following as a guideline:

- Use small talk to lead into other discussions. People love to talk about themselves. When in doubt, ask, "So, what do you do?"

- Always be well-groomed.

- Don't monopolize the conversation. Talk twenty percent of the time and listen eighty percent.

- Be outgoing and express interest.

- Volunteer your services, but never make promises you can't keep.

- Find a common ground and build on it.

- Follow up on an invitation to lunch or coffee.

- Never say anything negative about your competition.

- Remember names and use them. Everyone loves the sound of their own name.

- At a cocktail party, be careful not to get tipsy.

- Never flirt with a member of the opposite sex, even if you're both single. And *especially* if you're not.

- Remember at all times that you are representing your business.

Write and Submit Articles

To gain exposure for your wedding-planning business and establish yourself as an expert in your field, write articles about wedding planning.

Many wedding-related Web sites regularly ask for article submissions. They will sometimes specify the length of the article. If they don't, try to keep it between four and six paragraphs. Anything shorter may not provide enough information. Anything longer may not hold the reader's interest. With more and more brides surfing the Internet, you are sure to get a wide audience. Best of all, your article will be linked to your Web site.

Wedding magazines sometimes accept unsolicited material. Call the editor ahead of time to find out if they do and what the restrictions are. Generally speaking, if a magazine pays for your article they own the rights to it.

Your article must be full of information that you are sharing, not information on yourself or your business!

Write an E-Zine or
E-Mail Newsletter

An e-zine is an electronic magazine. It can be a colorful addition to your Web site, or it can be sent to brides-to-be in the form of an e-mail. This is probably the best way to get repeat visitors to your Web site.

When determining how often you will publish your e-zine, consider that the average bride will return monthly until her wedding, and then unsubscribe. Before committing yourself to writing a monthly newsletter, take a look at your personal schedule. If necessary, try a bimonthly, or even a quarterly issue.

Make it easy for readers to subscribe. The best way is to insert a line on your Web site that reads:

To subscribe to our wedding-planning newsletter, <u>click here.</u>

The underlined words will form a link to your e-mail, with "subscribe" in the subject line. Use this html, substituting your e-mail address for mine:

<a href="mailto:sandcastles@sharibeck.com?subject=Subscribe">click here</a>

E-mail newsletters can be sent out in plain text format or html, which allows colors, fonts, and pictures. To ensure that the newsletter will be seen the way you intend it to be, press the enter key when you are getting close to sixty characters.

Once your e-zine or e-mail newsletter has been written, how will you get it to your readers? If they will be viewing it on your Web site, set up the appropriate

links and upload the page. If you want to make it available only to those who
have subscribed, install a "password gate" onto your Web site.

As your subscription list grows, use a service such as Listserve, which allows
you to send your newsletter to a group of 100 or 100,000 with a single click.

Direct Mail

Direct mail advertising involves sending letters and postcards to every name that
appears on a mailing list. The mailing lists are made available when you advertise
in certain wedding magazines or participate in a bridal show.

Direct mail has the advantage over unsolicited mail, as it is addressed specifi-
cally to the bride. When she opens your mailing, you have her undivided attention for a full *three seconds!* She will either throw it out or take a closer look,
depending upon how you have designed it.

Many wedding planners send a brochure. Others prefer to enclose a flyer or
letter. The advantage of the flyer is that it takes less time to read. The bride will
be able to see at a glance if she is interested. You may wish to entice her by enclos-
ing a gift certificate.

The letter addresses the bride personally, and consists of three paragraphs in
which you briefly describe your business. Remember, sell benefits and invoke
emotion! Include a postscript in which you invite her to visit your Web site.

The major disadvantage to direct mailing is the cost of the printing, envelopes
and postage. Many businesses use postcards instead, but it is not as elegant.

Gift Certificates

Gift certificates can be used with many different promotions, and are a very effective way to attract business. You can issue them in one of two ways:

- a free service, such as a one-hour consultation
- a specific amount, such as twenty-five dollars, redeemable toward any
  product or service

Gift certificates make great prizes at a bridal shows. You may wish to have a
draw at your booth for a fifty-dollar gift certificate. The bride will most likely
spend it on a consultation, after which she may be so impressed that you will be
able to count on additional business from her.

It is recommended that a gift certificate have an expiry date. It creates a sense of urgency in the bride, and she will come to you sooner rather than later.

You can buy blank gift certificates at any business supply store. They usually come three to a page, which you can print on your computer. Don't forget to add your logo, and present it in a matching envelope.

Giving Interviews

Your local cable station may be interested in doing a human interest piece about your business. You will be given the line of questioning ahead of time so that you can prepare your answers. In some cases, viewers are invited to phone in and ask questions. Be sure to wear something colorful but not too bright. Never wear narrow stripes, as they tend to strobe. If you are nervous, keep your hands gently clasped on your lap. Cross your ankles, never your legs. Make it a point to speak slowly. Radio interviews are easier, since you know you won't be seen. Again, when you are nervous you may need to remind yourself to speak slowly.

If you are being interviewed for print, either in a magazine or a newspaper, you must still choose your outfit carefully, as the article will most likely be accompanied by a photograph. Print interviews differ from live interviews in that the interviewer returns to the office to rewrite the notes into a finished story. Not everything will necessarily be used. Some of the wording may change, and you might find yourself quoted in a slightly different way than you actually intended. Don't worry; the reading public will never know. All that matters is that they spell your name correctly and mention the most important points. Be sure they print your telephone number. You are bound to get many telephone calls when the story is printed!

As a rule, stories get printed if they are newsworthy or of public interest. When you first open your business, call your community paper and ask them to write a story. After you have been in business for some time, you can do things to get into the paper again. For example, you will get publicity if you are planning a wedding for a local celebrity. Or, you may hold a seminar on wedding planning and donate a portion of the proceeds to charity.

Yellow Pages Advertising

Advertising in the Yellow pages is a very efficient use of your marketing dollar. For a home-based business, it is the number-one reason to get a business telephone. The Yellow Pages are present in the phone books of every geographic area. In very large cites, they occupy a separate book. It is a well-known fact that brides look in the Yellow Pages when they are ready to buy.

- They will consult the Yellow Pages to help locate a wedding planner, and call you as a result.

- They will remember seeing or hearing about you, and will use the Yellow Pages as a quick way to locate you.

If you have a business telephone, you are entitled to a free one-line listing in your local Yellow Pages. There is an additional charge for a larger ad, bold type, or placing your listing in the Yellow Pages of another city.

If you look through "Wedding Planning" listings in your local directory, you will see how the one-line listings get lost among the larger ads. Look at the pages as if you were a bride ready to hire a wedding planner. Which ads would you respond to? Look at the content of the larger ads. Some feature artwork or photographs, others list their services, and still others offer promotions. Examine each one closely and use what you have learned to design your ad.

Some of the ads have a cluttered, "busy" appearance. Most people tend to put too much into their ads. Advertising professionals tell us that for an ad to stand out on the page it should have plenty of white space (empty space within the confines of its borders). Rather than including too much information, direct readers to your Web site.

Public Speaking

There are many instances in which a wedding planner may be asked to deliver an address. For example, a local business women's club may find it interesting that you plan weddings for a living and want to hear more. Here are some hints to ensure your success:

- Don't be afraid of your audience. They are not there to prove you wrong, but rather to learn from you. You are the expert, and they are grateful to you for answering their questions.

- Practice in front of family and friends and ask for feedback. Record yourself and examine your gestures, body language, and voice.

- Don't memorize your entire speech, as it will sound less natural. If you know your subject and have memorized your outline, you should be able to keep your notes to a minimum.

- Use overhead transparencies or slides.

- Involve the audience. Their feedback will keep things fresh and loose.

- Wrap up a little early so that you will have time to answer questions.

Write a Book

This is not a job for the faint-of-heart, but it is a way to add to your income. There are only so many geographical areas in which you can conveniently plan weddings. Brides in other areas can become a source of business if you sell them your book of wedding-planning tips. Or, you may wish to adapt recipes for large groups and turn them into a book on catering your own home wedding.

Once you have an idea for your book, set up a chapter structure and begin placing ideas and notes within each. The actual process of writing your book should take six months to a year. When the book is completed, you can have it picked up by a publisher, or you can produce copies on your own.

Publishers are not always eager to take a chance on a first-time author, and save their marketing for well-known names. You must promote your own book. The publisher will have the cover designed, often with your input. They will reserve the right to make changes to the name and copy in order to make the book sell better. You will receive royalties on each book sold, according to your contract.

When you print your own books, you pay for the printing and binding at your local copy center. Anything left over is yours to keep. The easiest type of binding is cerlox binding. It involves punching the pages and inserting the teeth of a plastic spine. An alternative would be to have the pages inserted into a three-ring binder, with an attractive cover. This would work especially well for the recipe book we mentioned earlier.

Have your book copyrighted. There is a fee, but the cost is nothing compared to having all of your hard work plagiarized.

Teach a Course

The quickest way to gain a reputation as an expert is to teach a subject to others. Many community colleges offer special interest courses; I taught such a course on interior decorating for seventeen years. You may wish to design a short course to teach brides how to better plan their weddings.

Contact the school and ask to speak to the person in charge of Continuous Learning. Tell them about your idea, and give them a brief description. Follow up with a detailed course outline by mail or fax. If they like what they see, they will probably want to interview you and offer you a contract. As a rule, your contract will begin the day of your first class and end the day of the last class. You will sign another contract if your course proves to be popular and is repeated.

Before submitting your proposal to the school, sit down and work out all the details. Things to consider are:

- length of course
- number of lessons
- topics to be covered
- brief description of each lesson
- audiovisuals to be used
- additional resources

Keep in mind that all materials you create in order to teach the course are the property of the school.

Since you must reserve Saturdays for weddings, arrange to teach the course in the evening. Don't make your students a captive audience as you try to get extra business. It is a conflict of interest for you to sign a contract with one of your students, but you can expect to get many referrals from them.

Word-of-Mouth Advertising

For better or worse, word-of-mouth advertising is the most effective of all. When it's good, it will bring you much business, but nothing can destroy your business as quickly as an unhappy bride. Bad news travels fast. For this reason, do everything you can to make every client rave about you.

Give a supply of your business cards to your husband, your family, and your friends. Ask them to hand them out to anyone they know who is getting married. But remember, promoting your business is your job, not theirs. Don't expect them to go around talking about you all the time. Be sure to write a thank-you note to former clients who refer you. That is the best type of testimonial!

We have all heard of businesses that don't need to advertise because they get so much word-of-mouth advertising. This is no exaggeration; it can actually happen. Get them talking about *you*!

For Your Notes

8

GAINING EXPOSURE THROUGH BRIDAL SHOWS

Are Bridal Shows Worthwhile For Wedding Planners?

The answer to that question is a loud "yes!" The bridal show can be one of your best marketing strategies *if* you know how to use it to your advantage. How can such a show benefit your business?

- The bridal show will give you the opportunity to meet more brides in one weekend than in years of consulting. Each bride you meet and speak with is a potential client.

- The bridal show will get the bride in the mood to talk with you about her wedding. She will feel none of the pressure she might feel if she were meeting with you at your office.

- The bridal show will give you the opportunity to network with other vendors.

- The bridal show will enhance your image in the eyes of the bride. She will see you as the professional you are!

- The bridal show will allow you to outshine the competition.

- The bridal show will provide you with a list of brides, as well as their addresses and telephone numbers, so that you can follow up afterwards.

- The bridal show will let the bride realize that wedding planners are just as important to the success of her day as the florist and the DJ. In fact, she may not have considered hiring a wedding planner until she noticed your booth!

Types of Bridal Shows

To the casual observer, all bridal shows may seem more or less the same, except perhaps for their size. As a wedding planner, you have a much wider perspective. There are two main types of bridal shows, the local and the national. Within the category of local shows there are exclusive shows and open shows. Naturally, each has its pros and cons. It is important to weigh each of these factors before deciding if the show is right for you.

You may already be familiar with the national bridal show. These are held in large cities, usually in the largest venue in the city. They offer aisle after aisle of the most beautiful wedding gowns, cakes, invitations, and services any bride could hope for. They also have the greatest number of people attending, and the largest advertising budgets. That translates into more exposure for their vendors. That exposure comes at a price, as these are the most expensive shows in which to participate. The main advantage to this type of show is consistency. The shows are professionally produced, and each is of the same quality, whatever its location. The models are professional; they either travel with the show, or return to the show whenever it is in their city. Wedding planning is such a locally-based business that the extra cost of a national show may not be justified. On the other hand, the extra exposure due to advertising and high attendance may be just what your business needs.

The local bridal show will showcase businesses from your immediate area, rather than businesses that are nationally-known. These shows are naturally less expensive, as you will not be paying for nation-wide advertising. At the same time, they may be a little less professional than you might like. Visit the show and see what you think of it. If you're impressed, you can participate in it next year.

Some bridal shows are exclusive. This means that you will be the only wedding planner there. Likewise, there will be only one DJ, florist, caterer, photographer etc. For this reason, the exclusive shows are more expensive. Visitors won't stay as long, as there is no opportunity for comparison shopping. It can also be difficult to get in; last year's wedding planner will be offered the first chance at a spot in this year's show. Having been lucky enough to have had an exclusive spot, I can honestly say it's worth it. Business owners who participate in exclusive shows are often very pleased with their yearly results. Consider, too, that exclusivity will enhance your image in the eyes of the public.

The bridal show most likely to attract the first-time exhibitor is the open show. These shows are produced locally and are often sponsored by prominent businesses in the area. They are the least expensive, but they can also be the least professional. Anyone calling herself a wedding planner is welcome to participate, so you may need to stand out in a crowd of competition. These shows are generally well-attended, and those attending usually live in the immediate area of your business. Often, if the show is sponsored by a local newspaper or radio station, the advertising alone can make it worth your while. In addition, there will be an opportunity to meet new vendors.

For the first-time exhibitor, I always recommend the open local show. It will give you a taste of the atmosphere and pace of a bridal show for the lowest financial investment. It will also bring you increased exposure in your community, both in the people you meet and in printed advertising.

Once you become a veteran of these shows, you may decide to move on to the national show. Or, you may decide produce a local show of your own; you will learn how in Chapter 9!

Offer Something for Every Bride

In order to get the most from your participation, you must be able to offer something for brides in each phase of planning, as we discussed in Chapter 7.

Anywhere from eight to twelve months before the wedding, the bride has just become engaged. She may not yet be aware that she needs the services of a wedding planner. Many a bride in this phase is determined to plan her own wedding, and may consider herself a failure if she is not able to do so. Explain that you can introduce her to the vendors and use your expertise to help her plan a stress-free wedding. Impress upon her that she will still have complete control of the wedding, and that her wedding will reflect her personality.

From six to eight months before the wedding, the bride is beginning to feel overwhelmed. Show her how she will benefit from having you help with some of the things that are causing her difficulty.

Three months before the wedding the bride has so much to do, and she may need your help to get it all done. You may also meet the bride who is finished her planning and is attending the show just for fun. Convince her that the wedding day is for family and friends. Neither she nor her mother should have any responsibility on that day. This bride needs your wedding day coordination.

The Contract

Your show contract may be several pages long and full of legalese, or it may be shorter and quite straightforward. It depends on the type and size of the show. You are responsible for all items in the contract, whether you understand them or not. Always have a lawyer look over the contract before you sign it. You must be familiar with several issues:

COSTS:

Have everything itemized, and be sure there are no hidden expenses.

GUARANTEES:

What guarantees will you receive from the show's producer? This could include any number of other items. Do you get the right of first refusal for the next show?

DEPOSITS AND PAYMENTS

How much is the deposit? When is it due? As a rule, it is due upon the signing of the contract. What are the amounts and due dates for further payments? What happens if you are late with your payment? Often the fine print says that your booth can be rented to someone else.

YOUR BOOTH AND EXHIBIT:

What are the sizes of the booths? Can you choose your booth? Can you change your choice afterward? Do you have complete control over your booth? Can you share a booth with someone else? What is included in the booth fee?

ADVERTISING:

What kinds of advertising are planned? Ask to see examples. Will you be mentioned by name? What media will be used?

SET-UP AND TEAR DOWN:

When can this be done, and by whom?

CONTACT LIST:

When will you receive it? How will the list be organized (by name, by wedding date, by geographic location)? What information will be on the list?

EXTRAS:

Do you have access to the vendor lounge? Is there an extra charge for this?

FASHION SHOW:

Is a contribution to the fashion show mandatory?

DOOR PRIZES AND DRAWS:

What is the dollar figure that you are expected to donate for the door prize? What is the registration process for brides entering the draw? Can you have a draw at your own booth?

CANCELLATIONS—YOURS:

When is the last date to cancel without penalty? What if you get sick at the last minute or if there is a death in your family? Can you get your deposit back if your booth can be rented to someone else? As a rule, you will lose your deposit, and be careful—sometimes the fine print states that you can be fined for not showing up!

CANCELLATIONS—THEIRS:

If the show is cancelled, do you get back your deposit and other payments you made? Probably not, so you are best to go with a producer who has a good track record.

Budgeting

Until your contacts turn into contracts, every aspect of your participation in the bridal show is an expense. Keep track of the figures, as you will need them after the show to conduct your analysis. For now, ask yourself, "Will participating in this show put too much strain on my cash flow?" If the answer is "yes," you may wish to start now to budget for next year. If you are able to manage it, go ahead. You may prefer to include show expenses in your advertising budget, because that's what they are.

Use this checklist to be sure you have included all of your expenses. In the space beside each item, keep track of the costs.

booth rental

pipe and draping

booth décor

electricity

rentals

furniture

display

truck rental

booth sign

brochures

business cards

handouts

booth prize

door prize

temporary help

fashion show fee

extra mileage to and from show

accommodation
other

Your Show Booth

Your show booth introduces your services in a tangible manner. Make it consistent with your personality.

Booths are usually 10 feet by 10 feet, or 8 feet by 10 feet. If you need a larger space, you may be able to rent two adjacent booths. Booths are often priced according to their location. End booths, booths near the fashion show, and booths to the right of the entrance usually cost more, due to their desirable locations. You may not be able to get the prime spots for your first few shows, as many organizers offer first choice to repeat exhibitors. Others operate on a first-come, first-served basis.

Research has shown that most people, when entering a store or a trade show, will turn to the right. This means that if you are located to the right of the entrance, brides will visit your booth earlier, before they have a chance to get tired. A booth at the end of an aisle is best, as you are exposed on both sides. This will allow you to create ways to enter and exit, thereby improving traffic flow. The back end of an aisle is not a good idea if it is a dead end. Many people don't bother to go all the way to the end. However, if that is your only option, make your booth so spectacular that guests will go out of their way to see it. The closer you can get to the fashion show, the better. Many brides come to the bridal show just to see the gowns, and you will benefit from the traffic past your booth as visitors enter and leave the show area. Although these prime spots are usually more expensive, in my experience they're well worth it.

Some bridal shows create a more open and airy feeling by eliminating the use of curtained booths. They place their vendors slightly farther apart, and are therefore not able to fit as many exhibitors into the same amount of space. This tends to raise the cost of a booth, but curtained booths are often unattractive and will leave you feeling claustrophobic by the end of the weekend.

If the show uses curtained booths, the booth fee usually buys you the metal frame only, although sometimes the curtains are included. You may be lucky enough to have a choice of curtain color, but this is not often the case. Find out what color the curtains are before you design the booth.

You are not likely to need help designing the show booth. Wedding planners are sufficiently talented and experienced in color and space planning to handle the job themselves. Keep it simple and elegant. Now is the time to be a perfectionist. If it's not flawless, don't have it in your booth. Use fabrics such as silks and velvets. Of course, your sign will be professionally-lettered. Furnish the booth with three chairs, one for you and two for your visitors. However, you will sit with visitors only briefly. As tiring as it is, you must stand to greet those who file past your booth. You will need a table on which to display your business cards and brochures. Display only a few at a time to make them seem more exclusive. Keep a box of each hidden under the table for replenishing. If you wish to display pictures of past weddings, be sure to get permission from former brides.

You will be responsible for having the booth wired for electricity. A contractor will be retained by the show's producer, and you are obligated to go through them.

If you sell or produce wedding-related merchandise, be sure to incorporate it into your booth. Depending on the fine print of the contract, you might not be permitted to actually sell your merchandise, but you can display it for advertising purposes.

Check your contract thoroughly. Each show is different, and something you read about in this chapter may not be permitted at your show. If anything in your booth is prohibited in the contract, the producer may reserve the right to remove you from the show. In this case, you will not get a refund.

Use the following checklist to ensure that you have not forgotten anything you will need for the day of the show:

- carpet
- arrange for electrical service
- table
- three chairs
- table lamp, to soften the effect of the overhead florescent lighting
- folding display, if needed
- décor items
- emergency kit, because headaches and pantyhose runs can happen anywhere
- items for retail sale
- cash box
- business cards

- brochures
- portfolio
- camera, to take a picture of your booth set up
- plume pen, and extra refills
- container and forms for booth draw entries
- appointment book

Marketing and Advertising

You will be included in the show's advertising. Your show fee is paying for it, so get the most from it. Don't wait passively for potential clients to read the ads and attend the show. Employ some of your marketing strategies to make it happen.

Send a letter to each couple with whom you have had contact, inviting them to come to the show and visit your booth. When consulting with new clients, offer them a pair of tickets.

Announce on your Web site that you will be at the show, and that there will be a special draw. In your print advertising, extend the invitation to "Visit us at the *World of Brides* Show, January 29, 20XX at Northview Conference Center."

If you belong to a networking group or your local Chamber of Commerce, let other members know that you'll be in the upcoming show. They may tell someone who is getting married.

First Impressions

The manner in which you greet visitors to your booth makes a difference in the way they will perceive you and your business.

Check your body language. If you fold your arms in front of you, visitors will get the message that you're unapproachable. If you don't know what to do with your hands, try holding a few brochures. That way, you are able to hand them out directly.

As tiring as it can be to stand on your feet all day, don't sit in your booth. People might think that you're bored. Stand up straight and smile, even if your feet are killing you! Don't stand behind a table; it will create a psychological barrier between you and your visitor. Stand in front of any furniture, at the very edge of your booth.

Don't eat at your booth. Someone may want to ask you a question, but they will hesitate to interrupt your snack. Coffee is okay—in fact, by the end of this show you will think that caffeine is a food group!

When talking to a couple, pay more attention to the bride than the groom. Wedding planners sometimes try too hard to appear outgoing, and give the impression that they are flirting with the groom. Don't ignore the groom, and answer all his questions, but smile more at the bride and make eye contact with her more often.

Pay attention to your appearance. You must be comfortable, but not too casual; stylish, but not too flashy; professional, yet not too aloof. Dress as if you were meeting a bride and groom for a consultation. A nice skirt or pants with a blouse or sweater would be perfect. The skirt should be neither too tight nor too short. Your shoes should have a heel height that is attractive for the length of your skirt, yet comfortable for standing. I always found it best to have several pairs of shoes with varying heel heights; it feels good to make a switch several times a day.

A few well-chosen pieces of jewelry are better than too many pieces. Avoid anything that jingles, as it is distracting and very unprofessional.

Posture is important. That's not so easy when you've been standing all day with another day ahead of you tomorrow. You will have to remind yourself constantly.

Smile—need I say more?

Most importantly, go to bed early the night before a show. You will need to be well-rested for the grueling day ahead. Be sure you have Tylenol in your bag, because nothing will affect your appearance like a headache.

Meeting the Public

As they enter the bridal show, visitors are given plastic bags in which to carry the many handouts they receive from the vendors. These often take the form of samples, to help the bride remember them long after the show is over.

A wedding planner doesn't have samples of her work, as many other vendors do, so think of something else. Choose a handout that fits your budget. Perhaps a silk rose or small packet of mints with your business card attached, or maybe a fridge magnet made from your card. Have a silver or crystal dish of mints in your booth for visitors to help themselves.

Give prospective clients your brochure. Keep plenty on hand, but only display a few. Psychologically, a brochure has more value if does not appear to be mass-produced. If you use a portfolio brochure, you may wish to design and print a less expensive one for bridal shows; double-or triple-folded brochures work well.

Don't have visitors pick up your brochure off a table. Hand it to them. The fact that you have physically handed the brochure to a bride and she has accepted it creates a psychological bond. Use this to your advantage.

Visitors to your booth will ask to see examples of your work. Have a wide variety in your portfolio, ready to show. Vary the formality, venue, and size of the weddings. Include some second weddings, to appeal to the older or second-time bride. You do not need permission from former clients to show your portfolio. However, framing pictures or hanging them on a display board is considered public exhibition, and requires the couple's written consent. The same is true if you want to play a DVD of one of your weddings.

If a couple seems ready to book a consultation with you, nothing will turn them off more quickly than if you said, "I'll call you next week to set something up." By the time you call, chances are they will have changed their minds. For this reason, have your appointment book at the booth. Before booking a consultation, check the wedding date to be sure you're available that day. If you have the date free, mark it with a question mark in pencil. This will alert you that there is a possibility of a wedding on that day. Of course, nothing is final until the contract is signed. If you are booked for that day, you may still be able to offer your services as a consultant.

Arrange a mutually-convenient meeting at your office or the couple's home. Print the date on the back of your business card and give directions. Have a supply of directions with a map printed on tasteful card stock—avoid cheap photocopies. As the clients leave your booth, be sure they have a brochure. That way, they can whet their appetites further, and they will have a better idea of what you offer.

Don't make the mistake of consulting with a bride and groom during the show. In the meantime, others will be passing your booth, and you will lose the chance to make contact with many potential clients.

The Fashion Show

The fashion show is the highlight of the weekend; it is the sole reason many brides attend. Local bridal and tuxedo rental companies are the main participants. Other wedding vendors can also contribute. The florist will make the bouquets carried by the models, and the DJ will provide the music.

As a wedding planner, there is not much you can do to participate. However, you may be able to think of ways in which you can offer your services to the producer:

- Provide the commentator with valuable information to use as filler, such as the fact that it was Queen Victoria who popularized the white wedding dress.

- Conduct the rehearsal. You already advise brides how to walk and move—it should be easier with actual models!

- Provide wedding-planning tips for the program.

Retail Selling

Many wedding planners supplement their income by selling wedding-related items to their clients. If you sell such things as plume pens, toasting goblets, and invitations as part of your business, by all means have a supply on hand to sell to those who visit your booth. Be sure to check your contract first, because retail selling is prohibited at some bridal shows.

Retail merchandise gives visitors a reason to stop at your booth. It gives them a reason to stay longer, allowing you to make that all-important contact with them. It is also a great way to introduce your services to them. If a couple places their invitation order at the show, you will see them again when the order is ready. By that time they may have realized that they can use your services.

If you don't usually carry such items, you may wish to sell them whenever you are doing a bridal show. They are a perfect way to fill your booth if you sell an intangible service. Make sure the merchandise you sell has the same degree of elegance as your business. Sell beautiful crystal toasting goblets, not the ones with "Bride" and "Groom" etched on them. Make sure your invitation line is of the highest quality.

Every time you make a sale, slip your business card and a brochure into the bag.

Door Prizes and Booth Draws

All vendors (that includes you) are expected to contribute to the door prize. In most cases it will be an item worth approximately fifty dollars or a gift certificate for the same amount. Vendors are occasionally asked to donate a certain amount of money toward one grand prize. Usually, though, the grand prize is donated by a large corporation, and may be anything from a honeymoon to a set of wedding bands. In return for your contribution, you get a contact list, compiled when brides register for the prizes.

When deciding what to donate, consider the nature of your business. If you contribute merchandise, the bride may not even remember who the donor was. However, a gift certificate for a free one-hour consultation will keep you at the front of her mind. You may end up with business you would not have had otherwise.

If you decide to offer a free consultation, remember the warning in Chapter 2. If you disillusion the bride by pitching your business instead of answering her questions, she will never hire you.

Many vendors hold their own draws for those who visit their booths. This has two advantages: it creates a second contact list and it allows you the opportunity to get to know the bride better. If a free consultation was your door prize, you should offer something different at your booth, such as:

- A book of wedding-planning tips, inscribed by you inside the front cover. Perhaps this is a book that you have written?

- A gift certificate for fifty dollars off wedding-planning fees

- A silver picture frame, in which you have displayed a reminder of your services, especially designed for the purpose

To register for the prize at your booth, have the bride fill out a preprinted card. The cards can be deposited into a glass bowl or other suitable container. You may wish to have the drawing during the last half-hour of the show. If the winner must be present in order to claim the prize, the law states that this must be printed on the ticket.

The Contact List

The greatest benefit of participating in a bridal show is the contact list you receive afterward. This list will give you the names of the bride and groom, the bride's address, telephone number, e-mail, and the date of the wedding.

It is imperative that you be in contact with these brides as soon as possible after the show, before they hire another wedding planner. The show's producer will make it a priority to give you this list within a week of the show at the very latest. If you had a booth draw you will have a list that slightly overlaps the first one.

Begin your direct mail campaign before the show. Have the flyer or letter designed, but don't print it until after the show, when you will know how many you'll need. Colored papers are best for flyers. Use delicate pastel colors. The letter should be on your business letterhead.

On the flyer, list the benefits the bride will enjoy if she hires you. Go for the emotional response by using such benefits as these:

- You will have more time to spend with your fiancé.

- You will have more time to spend on the "fun" parts of planning a wedding while you leave the other details to me.

- You will be free to enjoy your groom and your guests, while I take care of everything behind-the-scenes.

- You will save money … perhaps you will spend it on your honeymoon?

If you decide on both a flyer and a letter, mail the flyer first, and follow up with the letter about three weeks later. Be sure to add the cost of printing, envelopes and postage to your budget. Direct mail is expensive, but it is proven to be effective. To refresh your memory, refer back to Chapter 7.

Evaluating Your Success

It will take about six months before you will be able to judge whether or not your participation in the bridal show was a success. By that time you will have had contact (and probably *contracts*) with couples who met you at the show. You will have figured out the exact cost of the show, and you can weigh this against the added business you will see as a result.

Consider these other factors as well:

- How many weddings do you foresee booking in the next two years as a direct result of the show?

- What did you sell at your booth, and how much profit did you make?

- How many appointments have you made with show attendees, even through you haven't actually met with them yet?

- Have you heard from the winner of your door prize?

- Was the show well-attended?

Analyze your performance at the show. Make changes and adjustments in time for next year:

- Was your booth as efficient as it could have been?
- Did you get any positive feedback? Negative?
- Did you have enough brochures, business cards, handouts?
- Is there anything else you can think of?

When you arrive home after your first bridal show, you'll be so tired that you will *swear* you'll never do another! The pace is exhausting but the atmosphere is intoxicating; within a month you'll be planning to do it all again!

After you have done many shows, you might be ready to take the next step—to produce a show of your own!

For Your Notes

9

PRODUCING
A BRIDAL SHOW

The Decision to Produce

If your area has no annual bridal show, produce one of your own. Show the bride how she can get the most from her wedding-planning dollars by hiring local businesses. The publicity is incredible, but do this only if you have the stamina!

It's not an impossible dream, but there are some things you must consider. When you rent a booth at a bridal show you have one weekend in which you are unavailable for clients, but producing a show means involvement on a much grander scale. You will be spending a great deal of time organizing and promoting the show. Can your business stand this? You can plan to see a modest profit, but the main benefit to producing the show will come to you in the form of a higher profile.

Venue and Timing

Every January, national bridal shows are held in most major cities. The new gowns that were ordered in the fall have now been delivered and are ready to show to the public.

Don't hold your show during January, February, or March if you live near a large city. There is no way you can compete with these national shows. On the other hand, the advertising paid for by the larger shows puts brides into the wedding-planning mood, so if your market is not too competitive and you are not located too close to the city, you can use this to your advantage.

The planning for a winter show will take place over the Christmas season, when you and your vendors are stressed enough. If you hold a show in February, you may have trouble finding a florist to participate, as they are busy filling orders for Valentine's Day. Spring shows are very successful for booking new clients, but spring is a busy time of the year for wedding planners. During the summer months, brides are on vacation, and you will have many weddings.

If you plan to take advantage of the national shows' advertising, time yours to coincide with the fall shows. Hold it in September or October. After the summer, until the Christmas season begins, there is a lull in the consumer market. Bookings made at a fall show will generally be for a spring wedding.

After you have planned the month, on which day of the week will you hold the show? Obviously, weekends are best, but I don't recommend an entire weekend. It's one thing to be an exhibitor in a show that runs for a weekend, but it's entirely different to be the producer of one. The longer the show runs, the harder the work and the more expensive it becomes. Leave that for the professional producers! If the show will be held on a Saturday, 11:00 or noon is a good time to open, and you can stay open later. Sundays are often better than Saturdays, as this will minimize the time your vendors must close their businesses in order to participate. Have the show open around 1:00, so as not to conflict with church services.

Determine if the geographical area can support a show. Couples will usually drive a reasonable distance to attend one of the larger shows, but they may be reluctant if you will be featuring fewer vendors. Use the market analysis you prepared in Chapter 1 to be sure your planned location is feasible. If you find that the area contains mostly retirees or families with young children, you may want to move the show elsewhere.

In choosing the venue, one of your first considerations will be the size of the show. That will be determined by the number of vendors you anticipate. You will likely find that the best spot for your show is a banquet hall.

Once the venue is chosen, there are unique factors to consider. Rental fees vary greatly. The more vendors you feature, the more income you will generate. Some venues offer better facilities than others. Check for such things as

- Changing rooms for the models, both male and female, and access to the stage area from these rooms.

- A smaller room for vendors to use as a lounge.

- Availability of the rooms the night before, so that the bulk of the work doesn't need to be done in a rush the morning of the show. If the rooms are not available, can storage be provided overnight?

- Does the site provide audio-visual equipment? If not, what are the restrictions on the music you will be providing?

- Are a stage, runway, and risers available, or do you have to rent these?

- Can you serve coffee and refreshments?

Examine your needs carefully and address your concerns before you sign the contract. As the signer, you are financially responsible for everything, including the deposit. Get a deposit from your vendors ahead of time so as not to create a cash-flow problem within your business.

You will forfeit your deposit if you must cancel your contract with the venue. Develop a clear policy regarding vendors' deposits. Unfortunately, this is a lose/lose situation. If you return the deposits you will suffer a financial loss. If not, your reputation will suffer, not to mention your future relationships with these vendors. Do your research very carefully before signing anything.

Legal Considerations

Before the planning process gets underway, these items need your consideration:

- You may need a permit to operate your show. Check with your local by-law office. If any of the exhibitors will be outdoors (such as a tent rental company), you must check local zoning by-laws as well.

- If you are considering a venue without its own catering or kitchen facilities, check the local regulations regarding the preparation and serving of food.

- In some localities, union contracts are set up to protect workers, such as electricians. Be sure to find out all you can, as this affects your set-up.

- Find out if there will be a need for extra security. This will add to your cost and will be passed on to the vendors.

- What about garbage removal?

- Will your show create the need for additional parking arrangements?

- Find out ahead of time if your state or province requires tax to be charged on the tickets.

- Before you do any mailings to advertise your door prizes, be sure to find out what local regulations say about using the mail to advertise raffles and prize drawings.

Financial Matters

As the show's producer, your main concern is finances. Without knowledge of your expenses, you cannot determine the fees your vendors will pay to participate. You cannot invite vendors to participate until you are able to tell them how much it will cost and what they will get for their money. Your answers to their questions may very well determine if they accept or decline.

On the following list, note all expected costs. Subtotal your expenses, and add ten percent for contingencies. This will give you the grand total.

Venue rental $ —
Vendor lounge $ —
Permits (if needed) $ —
Advertising $ —
Postage (for mailings) $ —
Security $ —
Coffee or refreshments $ —
Tickets $ —
Music $ —
Flowers/decoration $ —
Programs $ —
Payment to workers $ —
Handouts $ —
Traffic control $ —
Garbage disposal $ —
Vendor name tags $ —
Door prize tickets $ —
Model's fees $ —
Rentals $—
Other $—

Subtotal
Add 10% for contingencies
Grand total

Grand Total: $ divided by number of booths   = $ per vendor

Estimate the number of vendors. How many booths will the venue allow, leaving plenty of aisle space and room for the fashion show? To determine the fee for each vendor, divide your grand total by the number of booths.

Most bridal shows charge admission, but some are free of charge. Surprisingly, there doesn't seem to be much difference in the number of brides attending.

Today's bride is not afraid to spend money, as long as she gets value for her dollar. An admission fee doesn't scare her, but you will see more of the general public if there is no fee.

You must decide whether to charge admission to the fashion show, but do not charge twice. If there is no show admission charge, by all means sell tickets to a fashion show. If the fashion show is free, I recommend having each bride reserve a seat for herself and one guest. This also allows you to provide a more accurate head count for the printer.

If you decide to charge a general admission fee, borrow a trick from the large national shows. Include a 2-for-1 ticket in your printed advertising. The success of the bridal show depends upon the number of brides in attendance. If a bride can bring her fiancé, mother, or maid of honor to the show at no charge, she is more likely to attend.

Those who buy tickets in advance should get a slightly lower price than those who pay at the door. Give each vendor a supply to keep in their place of business. In your advertising, include a list of locations at which tickets can be purchased. The additional walk-in traffic will be a bonus for your vendors.

Advertising, Publicity, and Media Coverage

Develop the advertising strategy early in your planning. So many other things depend on the costs of advertising, and you need a plan before you can arrive at a dollar figure. You cannot calculate a cost per vendor until you have your advertising budget in place. As well, vendors will want to see your advertising plans before they decide to participate in the show.

The demographics of your area will greatly influence your choice of media. Without a target audience in mind, you cannot begin to plan your advertising.

Television advertising is the most expensive, and suitable only to the large shows. Networks will show your ad across a wide geographic area. This means that you are paying to reach people too far away to attend your show. If you are interested in television, consider the local cable stations. A bridal show is the kind of news story they are always looking for; they may do a feature story on you!

Call your local radio station; they may do a special spot in which several events in the same area on the same day are mentioned. Or, you may choose to provide copy to the DJ, who will read it over the air, for much less than a radio commercial would cost.

In the category of print, newspaper advertising is specifically-targeted and less expensive. Many papers publish a bridal section once or twice a year. If the timing of your show allows you to take advantage of this, by all means go ahead.

Add a page to your Web site, dedicated to the bridal show. Update it as needed, and include any information that the public needs to know. Add a link to your e-mail, in case they have any questions. Include your Web site address in all advertising, so the public can find out more.

Flyers are a cost-effective way to advertise the show. Many newspapers deliver flyers along with their papers. Or, perhaps you know a young person who would like to earn a little extra money. Municipalities often prohibit posting flyers or leaving them under the windshield wipers of cars. Flyers are often discarded without being read. Make yours eye-catching without being too loud. List the benefits of attending the show. If you put your Web site address on the flyer you won't have to crowd all that information onto it.

Publicity is free advertising, and takes place before the show. Media coverage is publicity that takes place at the show. Both usually take the form of a newspaper article that has been written about your bridal show. To arrange for coverage, contact the assignment editor of the newspaper. Be sure to follow up. Have yourself listed in their reference file, and give the assignment editor your business card. Advertising with a particular publication does not entitle you to coverage or publicity. Many amateurs remind the editor repeatedly that they are paying advertisers, which is so unprofessional that the editor will often drop the story.

Smaller cable television stations and local radio stations may also agree to provide coverage. This is especially true if a portion of the proceeds are to be donated to charity.

See Chapter 7 for more information on advertising.

Naming the Show

Before you can begin to design your advertising, you must decide on a name for the bridal show. Here are some ideas:

- Bridal Extravaganza
- Brides, Brides, Brides!
- Love is in the Air
- Bridal Spectacular
- Wedding Bells

- Weddings Unlimited
- Bridal Showcase
- Wedding Expo
- Making Memories
- Wonderful World of Weddings
- Beautiful Brides

Be careful not to give the show a name that is too "cute." Remember that you are trying to achieve an atmosphere of glamour and elegance. Check to see if the name is already in use at a show near you.

Increasing Attendance

Many factors determine whether a bride will choose to attend a bridal show. Some involve a conscious decision, others do not.

A conscious decision may be based on whether the bride sees value for the cost of her admission fee. Will she get to see a fashion show? Is the door prize something she can use?

The unconscious decisions are based on such things as the attractiveness of the show. Brides are particularly sensitive to beauty, and a show in an unattractive location, or one that skimps on the fancy trimmings, will not interest her.

Although the time of year may put you in competition with the national shows, if yours is the only show in town, it will still be well-attended. The bridal pool may be smaller, but the interest will be there.

A direct mail campaign may help increase show attendance. More details about direct mail can be found in Chapter 7. The names on your mailing list can come from many sources:

- the contact list from a previous show in which you have participated (be sure it's recent)
- customer lists from the vendors who will be renting booth space at your show
- potential clients who have called your business for information
- current clients of your wedding-planning business

The mailing gives the reader the important details of the upcoming bridal show and personally invites her to the fashion show. It can be in the format of a flyer or a wedding invitation. Be sure to list the benefits of attending the show; brides are best sold on emotion. Offer an incentive, such as a certificate for 2-for-1 admission. Enclose a reply card so you will know how many will be attending the fashion show. Set the response date for one month before the show. To request a reply, enclose a card that can be mailed back to you. Call your post office for information on "business reply" mail. That way, you will pay postage only on the replies that are returned.

The second mailing, sent out three weeks before the show, will take the form of a letter and will be personally signed. It will be mailed to brides on your list who have not yet purchased tickets or responded to your previous invitation.

The Venue Contract

After you have done your homework and chosen a venue for your bridal show, contact the location's sales representative. Ask if the date you prefer is still available, or if they can accommodate you on a different date. Find out if there is another function on the same date. This will affect everything from parking to security. Book a venue that is geared to the size of your crowd. If the group is smaller than the facility will accommodate, they are well within their rights to rent the unused space to someone else.

The contract will outline the financial aspects of the agreement: the total cost, the deposit, and the balance due. It will detail what you will get for your money, what you must pay extra for, and what restrictions you are expected to follow. Some of the details you must investigate are

- outdoor displays for tent rentals and limousines
- set-up requirements and union regulations
- availability of the location for the rehearsal of the fashion show
- set-up and tear-down times (the day before the show is the best time to set up)
- serving coffee or refreshments
- security and parking
- garbage removal
- capacity of the room

- any restrictions on individual booths
- items which are included, such as staging, chairs, booth draping, etc.

The room is not yours until you have signed the contract and paid your deposit. Work with reasonable speed on this task, but do not allow yourself to be rushed; you are responsible for the terms of this contract after it has been signed. Clarify any item that is questionable, and ask to change any item that is unacceptable. Before you sign a legally-binding contract, have your lawyer look it over.

Some things are negotiable, others are not. It depends on the venue and the request itself. Many venues realize that your bridal show is good advertising for them, and will be willing to bend.

The Show Vendors

The first place to look for vendors is your own business. The vendors you work with regularly already know you and your reputation, and will most likely want to participate in your show. If you want to include vendors you don't know, look in the Yellow Pages. Go through the listings and make several choices for each category. Look for recognizable names, good reputation, and quality. A second-rate vendor can cast a shadow on your own reputation.

Write a letter on your business letterhead. Introduce yourself and invite the vendor to participate in your bridal show. Outline the advantages of renting a booth. Send the letter to every vendor who interests you, and mention that you are operating on a first-come, first-served basis. Within two weeks, you should have received a response. If not, follow up.

If you get a rejection, don't take it personally. Many vendors are not interested in smaller shows, or may be unable to participate for any number of reasons. Although there are many listings in the Yellow Pages, only a few of them will be possible exhibitors.

Many bridal shows offer exclusives. This means that each vendor has no competition at the show. If you offer exclusives, you will need less space for booths and you will have a much easier job planning the show. The main disadvantage is that brides will have no opportunity for comparison shopping. As a final consideration, think of your own business. You work with more than one vendor in each category—how will exclusives affect your working relationship with those you do not include?

If you plan to offer exclusives, list your first, second, and third choices in each category. A personal visit or a phone call is the best way to contact your first choice. They will have questions and you must have answers. They may be a little wary if you are producing for the first time; address their concerns. If they are uninterested, contact the next vendor on your list.

Go to your meetings armed with statistics. Begin with your demographic and market analysis. Add to this the number of weddings that take place in your area, broken down by month and season. You may wish to prepare a presentation, complete with colorful graphs, to demonstrate your professionalism and the amount of research you have done.

Be able to tell exactly how many people the venue will hold. Explain that for every bride there are 2.5 "others," such as grooms, mothers, or maids of honor. Florists, jewelers, and caterers can expect future business through them.

Talk about the exposure they will gain from being in your show. They will be meeting more brides in one weekend than they would anywhere else. They will be featured in all advertising. Be specific as to how much advertising will be done, and in which media. You may be asked to show some of your preliminary advertising ideas.

In your enthusiasm to book a vendor, don't promise what you can't deliver. Don't speak in terms of dollars or volume, because you can't predict if any of the brides who come to the show will end up as clients. That depends on the vendors themselves.

Vendor Mix

Have a good mix of vendors. Nothing will undermine the success of your show more quickly than a frustrated bride who expects one-stop shopping and doesn't find it. The vendors want as much exposure as possible. Many will be willing to provide merchandise or services free of charge for the fashion show in exchange for advertising in the show program and the commentary. This should be optional, except for the bridal salon that rents a booth; their participation is expected. To achieve a pleasing vendor mix, include each of the following categories:

WEDDING GOWNS

Since the wedding gowns are the stars of the fashion show and the reason many brides attend, choosing the salons and dress shops is of the utmost importance. Meet several times with the owners and staff to choose the featured gowns. Be sure to get pictures and descriptions of each, so the florists can provide the perfect flowers. Determine all accessories needed. If this vendor cannot provide them, arrange for a separate vendor for accessories. The store may choose not to have a booth, but to be involved solely with the fashion show.

FORMAL WEAR

Tuxedo rental companies usually rent booths in addition to providing the fashion show with tuxedos for the groom, best man, ushers, fathers, and ring bearer. Be sure that all accessories are also available. Have the florist provide boutonnieres.

HAIR STYLISTS AND MAKEUP ARTISTS

These businesses often book appointments soon after the show, and are strong possibilities. In addition, they may be able to do the hair and makeup for the models.

DISC JOCKEYS

The DJ will also provide the music for the fashion show. They often want to play music at their booth. It is up to you to develop a policy on this issue. I prefer not to have it, for two reasons. First, it is sure to disturb other vendors. Secondly, if the DJ plays a song by Elton John, it is an indication of Elton John's talent, not the DJ's.

BANDS AND ENSEMBLES

On the other hand, I would recommend allowing a band to demonstrate their music and style to visitors. In order not to disturb the neighboring vendors, have the music on several iPods or mp3 players. You may wish to have the band or ensemble play live at the fashion show.

FLORISTS

The florists who will be show vendors will provide the flowers for the fashion show. They may decide to produce silks instead of fresh flowers. That is their prerogative, as they may be able to use the bouquets for display or perhaps for sale.

PHOTOGRAPHERS

This will include still photography and videography. If you will allow wedding videos to be shown, insist that the volume be kept low.

RECEPTION VENUES

Banquet halls, restaurants, and hotels may be willing to provide representatives at their booths, where they will hand out brochures. Before renting a booth to them, check your contract for a conflict of interest clause. For example, if your show is in a hotel, you may be in conflict of interest if you allow another hotel to participate and advertise.

CATERERS

Caterers love bridal shows, as catering is one of the largest expenses incurred when planning a wedding.

LIMOUSINE RENTAL

Depending on the venue, it may be possible to display a limousine inside the show. If not, perhaps it can be parked outside. Check local by-laws that may prohibit outside exhibitors.

TENT RENTAL

The same applies to tent rental companies. If they are unable to set up a tent outside, they may opt to rely on printed material.

OTHER TRANSPORTATION

Horse and buggy rides from the ceremony to the reception are charming and popular. If such a company is in your area, they are sure to be interested. The same applies to vintage cars.

RENTAL SERVICES

As well as offering a large selection of rental items to booth visitors, the rental company may be able to provide necessities for the fashion show, such as folding chairs and even décor. In addition, they may be willing to provide (at no cost or at a discount) items that will add ambiance to the event, such as a fountain.

BAKERS

Bakers usually display a Styrofoam model of a wedding cake. Sometimes, they have visitors taste a sample of their cake. Check the local regulations regarding serving food at the venue.

JEWELERS

Many couples who visit bridal shows have not yet chosen their wedding rings. For this reason, jewelers are anxious to participate.

TRAVEL AGENCIES

With so many couples still thinking about their honeymoons, you should have no trouble signing a travel agent. They may even provide a door prize (for lots of publicity!)

BALLOON ARTIST

Balloons offer a great deal of impact for a relatively low cost, and have become popular for the bride on a budget. Again, here is a source of decorations for the fashion show.

WEDDING PLANNERS

If you plan a booth for your own business, will you also allow your competition to participate? You could end up with a damaged reputation, and even legal bills, if another wedding planner wants to rent a booth and is turned down (unless you offer exclusives). Don't invite another wedding planner into your show, but don't turn one down, either.

OTHER VENDORS

Local wedding-related businesses, such as dressmakers or even butterfly/dove releases can be included.

Vendor Contracts

The vendor contract will spell out your rights and obligations and those of the vendors. Once your signature is on that document, you are legally bound to deliver under its terms. Therefore, I always recommend that you send two unsigned copies to the vendor to sign and return to you. Only then will you sign them, returning one to the vendor. That way, no changes can be made without your approval.

The contract should include the following:

COSTS: Have everything itemized; do not hide expenses.

GUARANTEES: As the producer, what guarantees will you give the vendor? For example, right of first refusal for the next show, minimum number of attendees, and any number of items.

DEPOSITS AND PAYMENTS: The amount of the deposit should be indicated. As a rule, it is due upon the signing of the contract. Indicate in writing when further payments are due, and the amounts. Spell out your policies for late payments.

BOOTH AND EXHIBIT: Remember all the items you looked for when you signed a contract for your first show and add them to this contract. What are the sizes of the booths? Can the vendor choose their booth? Can the vendor share a booth with someone else? Does the vendor have complete control over their booth? Are sales allowed? Remember all the items you looked for when you signed a contract for your first show and add them to this contract.

ADVERTISING: What kinds of advertising are planned? Be prepared to show examples. Will the vendor be mentioned by name? What media will be used?

SET-UP AND TEAR DOWN: When can this be done, and by whom?

CONTACT LIST: When will the vendor receive it? How will the list be organized (by name, wedding date, or geographical location), and what information will be on the list?

EXTRAS: Will there be a vendor lounge?

FASHION SHOW: For vendors participating in the fashion show, include clauses regarding the vendor's obligation to provide the fashions and attend the rehearsals.

DOOR PRIZES AND DRAWS: What is the dollar figure that the vendor is expected to donate for the door prize? Can vendors have their own draw at their booth?

CANCELLATIONS (THEIRS): When is the last date to cancel without penalty? What if the vendor gets sick at the last minute, or has a death in the family? Can vendors get their money back if the booth can be rented to someone else? Can vendors sublet their booth to someone else? If you plan to make the deposit partially refundable until a certain date, specify that all notification to you must be in writing.

CANCELLATIONS (YOURS): If the show is cancelled, do vendors get back their deposits and other payments?

DISCLAIMER: You must state that you are not responsible for cancellation or disruption caused by labor disputes or acts of God. Furthermore, you must state that you are not responsible for loss or injury to any vendor or employee, and that you accept no responsibility for loss or damage to their property.

CHANGES: Specify that all changes to the contract must be made in writing and initialed by both parties. Under no circumstances should verbal changes be permitted.

Items to Consider

Before you begin to contact vendors, consider how many booths you will provide. Don't forget that a large area must be devoted to the fashion show and the seating for it. The size of the booths will also determine their number.

Will you group similar vendors or separate them? Most vendors prefer the latter, and I agree with them. This gives each vendor a chance to stand out, and makes it less likely that a bride will confuse them with a competitor. Two or more vendors may wish to share a booth and split the costs. This will increase the chances that smaller businesses will enter the show.

Will your business have a booth? Naturally, you want the exposure, but don't even consider steeping inside your booth—you have to be everywhere, problem-solving and making last-minute decisions. On the other hand, you can't afford to lose the valuable advertising that can only come from having a booth. Find someone reliable to fill in for you, as it is impossible for the show producer to be stuck in any one place for any given time.

The considerate bridal show producer knows how much hard work the vendors put into their participation. One way to offer them a little extra is to have a vendors' lounge, where they can take a break. Build the cost of the extra room rental into the show budget.

Assemble a variety of experts to speak on their specialty. Depending upon the length of the show, have a speaker available in the morning and one in the afternoon. A weekend show could accommodate three or four speakers, but a Sunday afternoon show, just one. Use the area allotted to the fashion show, since the chairs and podium will already be set up. Book the speaker and the fashion show a reasonable time apart. In fact, you may decide not to book a speaker on that afternoon.

Give your speaker a time frame of twenty to thirty minutes. After a short talk on a chosen topic, open the floor to questions. It is a good idea to have questions ready, so there won't be any long periods of silence if the audience is too shy to ask. In my experience, though, this rarely happens!

Interior designers, travel agents, bridal registries, investment planners, and real estate agents are always popular choices for guest speakers. They will most likely have topics ready. Just in case, though, here are a few suggestions:

- Choosing the perfect tableware for your lifestyle

- Financial planning for couples

- Decorating your first home

- Honeymooning in Europe

- Down payments and mortgages

Estimate that five to ten percent of your visitors will bring children to the show. As a service, especially for those who will be attending the fashion show, you may wish to provide child care. Decide whether to charge for this service or make it complimentary. I suggest a nominal amount, which can go toward paying the staff.

The ideal spot for the child care area would be a smaller room just off the main exhibition hall. If that's not possible, partition a corner of the main space. Equip the area with a variety of safe toys for all ages; these can be borrowed from friends, family, and neighbors. Do not allow anything small enough to be choked on. Crafts are not a good idea, because of the clean-up. Be sure to provide a first aid kit. Have the parents sign a release form absolving you, your staff, and the venue of responsibility in case of an accident.

Security is always a concern with parents, and these days you cannot be too careful. This is especially true at a trade show, where children are constantly being picked up and dropped off, and where the families are not known to the staff. Have the parents sign their child in and out, so that your staff will have the parents' names in case they have to be paged. A digital photo should be taken of the parent and child upon drop-off. Do not allow the staff to release the child to anyone other than the parents in the picture.

The contact list is the reason many vendors participate in bridal shows. For a large show, registration for the door prize is done by computer. Vendors at these shows get their lists before they finish tearing down their booths. You may not be able to provide the lists this quickly, but you must make it a priority to supply them within a week of the show *at the very latest*. The bride must be contacted while the show is fresh in her mind, and before she has a chance to hire a competitor.

The following information must be on the list:

- bride's name
- address
- telephone
- groom's name
- wedding date

The list must be organized. Use one of the following approaches:

- alphabetically by bride's last name
- geographically by address
- chronologically by wedding date

Show Staff

As the show's producer, you have the responsibility of hiring enough staff and volunteers to get the job done well. The vendors might know someone who would be willing to work for a day or a weekend to earn some extra money. If not, place a small ad in your local newspaper.

Your helpers may be willing to volunteer their time if a portion of the show profits will be going to charity. Otherwise, expect to pay them. Decide on a flat fee or an hourly rate. When organizing your list of helpers, include the following positions:

TICKET SALES

You should have three people at this table. Choose people you know and trust. They will need a locking cash drawer, which will be skimmed regularly. The money will be deposited into the bank, or stored temporarily in a secure location.

REGISTRATION TABLE

You need three people to sit at the registration table. They are responsible for providing the brides with their tickets, and helping them register for the door prize.

GREETER

Have someone formally dressed to welcome guests as they enter.

DISTRIBUTORS

You need two people to hand out programs.

YOUR ASSISTANT

Your assistant must be someone you know well, as this is a fairly responsible position. Your assistant will be out on the show floor, ready to assist vendors or visitors. A set of two-way radios will keep your assistant in constant touch with you.

FASHION SHOW COORDINATOR

This is often the owner of the bridal shop, as the role must be filled by someone who is familiar with the gowns. The coordinator will stand just behind the curtains and will be responsible for having the models in the proper order and straightening their trains just before they step out onto the stage. You need two coordinators if models will be entering the stage from both sides.

MODELS

You need brides, grooms, bridesmaids and maids of honor, best men and ushers, parents of the bride and groom, flower girls and ring bearers. Real people come in all shapes and sizes. Have a few shorter and plus-size models, so that brides who do not have model-like figures will be able to visualize themselves in the gowns. Have a racial mix that is representative of the population. Older brides in the audience will enjoy seeing older models.

BACKSTAGE MANAGERS

This person is in charge of all that goes on behind the scenes of the fashion show. She is responsible for making sure that all gowns are on the correct racks and that each model has what she needs.

DRESSERS

You will need one dresser for every two models. They will answer to the backstage manager. Their job is to help the models dress and to bag the gowns after the show so that they can be returned to the store from which they came.

COMMENTATOR

As the show producer, you may prefer to act as your own commentator. You have been with the show from the very beginning. You, more than anyone, truly understand the very fiber of its being. Therefore, you will be able to deliver a commentary as no one else can.

CHILD CARE PROVIDER

You may already know people who are good with children and have CPR and first aid training. If not, contact your local daycare center and hire several of their teachers. You will probably need three people.

YOUR BOOTH

You need someone reliable and knowledgeable about the operations of your business. This person will stay in your booth throughout the show, greeting visitors, handing out your brochures, and answering questions. You must pay them yourself, not from the show's budget.

Registration for Prizes

A spectacular door prize will spice up your advertising and attract more visitors to the show. The national shows have grand prizes, such as all-expenses-paid honeymoons. These are donated by large corporations in exchange for advertising and an enhanced public image. The size of your grand prize cannot compare to this. However, one of your vendors may be willing to donate a wedding gown or limousine service for the day of the wedding.

In addition to the grand prize, there will be draws for door prizes. Every vendor is obligated to contribute a product or a gift certificate for a specific dollar amount. In exchange, they will be identified as the donor in all advertising and at the drawing. As consolation prizes, some shows give away flower arrangements and decorations from the fashion show. This is at the discretion of those who have provided them, with your approval, of course.

Vendors may wish to hold draws at their own booths to attract visitors, resulting in increased business. This also allows the vendor to compile a secondary contact list.

Some shows try to encourage brides to visit more vendors by requiring that tickets be validated (usually by using a hole-punch) at the various booths. In my experience, this distracts the vendors from marketing their services and products to those who are genuinely interested. Other shows have visitors sign up for prizes at the booths. Again, this is time-consuming on the part of the vendors and involves repeated writing on the part of the bride, although many have started using printed labels.

Another commonly-used registration method involves registering for the grand prize at the door, and for the smaller prizes at the booths. Usually the tickets are printed and numbered with the vendor's name on each. The bride can enter for the prizes that interest her. Since many vendors like to have draws of their own, this only adds to the confusion.

You have more control over registration if it is handled at the door. It is more difficult for anyone other than brides to register for prizes, or for brides to register more than once for the same prize. If you simply hand out numbered tickets to everyone who pays for admission, you lose that control.

The door prize registration cards will have spaces for the bride to fill out her name, address, telephone numbers (home and work), and the date of the wedding. A 3 x 5 card will hold this information comfortably.

Print disclaimers on the registration cards, tickets and advertising if you will be placing restrictions on the prizes. For example, if the winner must be present to win, or if each person can win only one prize, this must be clearly stated. Have your lawyer look over anything to do with the prizes. They qualify as raffles, and as such are subject to strict laws and regulations.

Types of Fashion Shows

There are two main types of fashion shows: the independent fashion show, and the one that is the feature of a bridal show. The independent fashion show stands alone. If other vendors are brought in, it is to provide flowers, music, or decorations. No vendors set up booths, although they may be mentioned in the program.

Independent shows are often held in banquet halls. If a show is large enough, producers will often choose an auditorium, for its stage and existing seating. Depending on the length of the show, there may be an intermission.

Fashion shows that are produced as the showcase of a bridal show are shorter, to allow guests time to visit each booth. Depending on the layout of the venue, the fashion show can be held in the same room as the booths, or in a separate but easily-accessible room.

Production and organization are similar for both types of show.

The Ambiance of the Fashion Show

If the fashion show has been successful, the bridal show has been successful—that's how important it is! Planning a fashion show is like planning a wedding. There will be small mistakes during the actual event, but good planning will make sure the audience is unaware of them.

Planning a fashion show requires superior organizational skills. You will be working with dozens of wedding gowns, several models, makeup and hair stylists, decorators, and musicians. The show will require split-second timing, as well as opportunities for spontaneous moments. Children usually provide these. When my daughter was four, she was invited to be a flower girl in a fashion show. Laura attended all the rehearsals, where she and the little ring bearer performed flawlessly. On stage, however, they didn't listen to the commentator, much to the delight of the audience! One of the models took Laura by the hand and guided her through her scenes. We still get a kick out of watching the video!

Many producers use themes; others think it's tacky. Use your own discretion, but be sure to keep it tasteful, elegant, and related to weddings and romance. It is usually best to feature a theme for one or two segments only, not for the entire show. Besides, you'll want to save some of your ideas for your next show! Here are a few to consider:

- Choose a theme from the season, such as "Christmas Romance," "Winter Wonderland," or "FALLing in Love."

- Have a sequence that features the latest Broadway show.

- Several sequences can feature different colors. Since this is not actually a theme, you can do more with it.

- Pay tribute to an era, such as 1940's Hollywood, Ancient Greece, Victorian England, or Renaissance France.

- Feature a tribute to the glamorous women of the past and the not-so-past, such as Princess Diana and Jacqueline Kennedy. Feature fashions based on their personal style. Use models who resemble them.

- Devote a segment to the older bride and the second-time bride.

Work with the DJ and set decorator to develop a mood for these themes. Keep in mind that not only do elaborate sets take too long to change, but they will also cut deeply into your budget.

Before you meet with the DJ or the band regarding the music, you must have planned out the segments of the fashion show, complete with specific songs. Ask the DJ about the legalities of playing music in public; a tariff applies to public performance. Likewise, if you plan to use a live band, check with the musicians' union about the payment of royalties.

Have the DJ or band leader physically inspect the location. They must be sure that the electrical supply is adequate for their equipment and they will be able to advise you on the placement of the speakers and microphones.

Begin the show with dramatic music. Popular music should be instrumental. Lyrics tend to be distracting, especially when a great tune has words that don't apply to weddings or romance. If the lyrics convey the theme, though, include them. Include a variety of musical styles. Traditional wedding music, 1940's dance music, Broadway hits, and easy listening music will give you a pleasant mix.

The decorations for the fashion show should be kept simple and elegant—the gowns are the real stars of the show. Colorful balloons may be festive, but for this application, I suggest black, white, gold, or silver. The florist will provide large urns of flowers, trees with twinkling lights, and topiaries.

Producing the Fashion Show

You are responsible for locating bridal shops that are willing to provide the gowns and veils, a men's formal shop to provide the tuxedos, and other vendors to provide the accessories. You will add credibility to the show if there are several vendors in each category. The shop need not be large enough to stock the gowns needed. It is sometimes possible to obtain them from the manufacturer for the purposes of the fashion show. Choose the shops with which you want to work, and allow them to say what they can do for you.

The main drawback is wear and tear on the gowns. Many models are quite careless; I've even seen them end up on the floor! Dry cleaning, or at least spot-cleaning, is often necessary. You must provide clean sheets to cover the floors, and the gowns must be transported in garment bags in a clean truck. The bridal shop will have to provide some of its staff to assist at the show. The fact that their best gowns will be out of the shop may necessitate the closing of the store during this time, and the resultant loss of business. Before the show, they must accommodate the models who come into the store for fittings. The shop owner is also responsible for writing a description of each gown. Regardless, the benefits are just too great to pass up, and all the hard work pays off in dividends for the bridal shop.

The participating bridal shop(s) may be able to provide models who have worked with them in the past. Most likely, though, you'll be responsible for hiring them. If your budget allows, hire professionals. If you decide to use non-professionals, hold auditions. Have the would-be models show up in full makeup, with their hair styled off the face. Don't choose all tall and slim models; have a mix of figure types. Have the girls audition by walking on the runway, turning twice. Choose your models on the basis of poise and posture, and be sure that they feel comfortable on the runway. If the show will feature fancy choreography, see how well they can dance and move to music.

If you decide to use models with a little more experience, consider modeling students. Your local modeling agency or school will be more than happy to comply, especially if you give them credit in the program. These schools tend to attract teenaged girls, so you may have to get your older models from other sources.

You will need fewer models if you have fewer on the stage at a time, but don't show your models one at a time to save money. Bridesmaids are best shown in pairs, mothers and fathers should be seen together, and the bride must be escorted by the groom or her father.

About four weeks before the show, contact the vendors who will be supplying the fashions and accessories. They will give you the descriptions that you will use in the narration and the program. Prepare this in the order in which the gowns will be shown, and type it separately from the filler. The filler consists of useful or interesting pieces of information. You may wish to give the audience some wedding-planning tips. Or, you might entertain them with the origins of our popular wedding customs. On another separate sheet type a list of the participating vendors and a one-minute introduction of their services.

The number of rehearsals you need depends on the size and complexity of the fashion show. I prefer to hold three. The first will be held approximately three weeks before the show. The models, fashion show coordinator, and backstage manager must all attend. By now, you will have an idea of the scenes, and this is your chance to iron out any wrinkles. Use this opportunity to ensure that no model is in two consecutive scenes, thereby avoiding a situation where there is too little time to change. Type up a sheet indicting each scene in chronological order, and the models in order of appearance.

As you talk the models through the scenes, they will walk through their parts. When I am rehearsing a wedding I use a floor length lace curtain, though which I run a ribbon. Tied around the bride's waist, it allows her to practice moving gracefully with a train. This works equally well for the models.

For the second rehearsal, two weeks before the show, get the DJ involved. If that is not possible, a CD of the music will suffice. Again, the models will run through each sequence, preferably twice.

One week before the show, hold a dress rehearsal. Everyone involved in the show must attend. It is not practical to have the gowns and tuxedos at this time, so use the lace curtains again. With lights, music, and narration, make this rehearsal as close as possible to the real thing.

Instruct each model to carry her bouquet in her right hand, by her side. This will give the guests an unobstructed view of the gown.

The Fashion Show Program

The fashion show program must have a professional appearance. Your local business supply store has papers designed just for this purpose. Programs can be photocopied or printed. You will pay more for each ink color you add. To save costs on a two-color program, have one color for the paper and a second color for the ink.

By now you know approximately how many brides will be attending the show. Print extra programs just in case.

Include the following in your program:

- A brief description of each gown (shorter than your narration), including the price. This point is very important to the bride. If the vendor resists giving a price, use the suggested retail. Have a small check box printed in the margin beside each, so the bride can mark her choices.

- Small ads for each vendor participating in the fashion show.

- Blank pages for the bride to take notes.

Proofreading is of the utmost importance. Have the bridal shop and tuxedo rental owners read over your descriptions of their merchandise. Let each vendor okay their advertising. Make it clear that once the program is printed, it's final.

It's Show Time!

The big day has arrived, and the backstage area is bustling with activity! The gowns have been brought in on racks. The garment bags have been labeled with the model's name, scene number, and gown number.

Each dresser will have a card for the models assigned to her. In chronological order, she will find the model's name, the scene number, the gown number and the accessories needed. This is tacked to the wall in that model's assigned space. As each scene ends, the model will return quickly to her space, where the dresser will be ready with the next gown she is to wear.

Have the models arrive an hour before the show begins. They are to have their hair styled beforehand, with the hair back and off the face. Absolutely no hairspray is to be used near the gowns, as it can damage the trims and sequins.

It goes without saying that there will be no eating, drinking, or smoking backstage or anywhere near the gowns!

When you step up to the podium, you will be glad you have three separate pages. You cannot begin to describe a gown until the model is on the stage, and even the most well-rehearsed fashion shows can feature slight delays. The three-page method will allow you to quickly fill a gap, and then return to the commentary without the audience noticing. Be sure to spread the vendor introductions evenly throughout the show.

Vendor Evaluations

Before the bridal show ends, distribute an evaluation survey on which the vendors can give you their feedback. This will help you make positive changes for the next show you produce. You will also be able to get an idea of which vendors might like to participate in another show.

Your evaluation should take the form of open-ended questions. As you remember from Chapter 2, multiple-choice questions are not as indicative, nor do they give suggestions for improvement. Keep it brief, only about five questions. Sample wording follows:

1. What did you find good about the show?

2. What did you find poor about the show?

3. What would you like to see changed?

4. What feature most impressed you?

5. Would you participate in another show with us in the future? Why or why not?

Bridal Show Planning Timeline

EARLY PLANNING:

- Design vendor registration forms
- Investigate possible venues
- Work out budget

EIGHT WEEKS BEFORE (or earlier)

- Begin to secure vendors
- Book venue
- Secure businesses to participate in the fashion show
- Book models for the fashion show
- Book a commentator for the fashion show, unless you will be filling this spot
- Get a commitment from the supplier of your grand prize
- Design print advertising

SIX WEEKS BEFORE

- Submit print advertising
- Send your first direct mailing
- Confirm with set-up companies (draping, electricians, etc.)
- Begin a list of vendors, and add to it as necessary

FOUR WEEKS BEFORE

- Begin to work on the fashion show programs by gathering information and descriptions of the gowns. This information will also be used in the narration
- Begin to work on the narration. Start with the gown descriptions. You can add some filler later on

- Check in with all of the vendors. Ask to see what they have done so far, and request changes in anything that does not meet with your approval
- Hire someone to work in your booth and familiarize them with your business
- Arrange to have the correct number of mirrors, racks, etc., backstage for the fashion show
- Hire show staff
- Arrange for backstage personnel for the fashion show
- Decide how brides will register for door prizes, and design appropriate tickets
- Check replies against your direct mailing list
- Arrange to rent risers and stage for fashion show, if venue does not provide them
- Arrange to rent tables for booths and folding chairs for the fashion show, if venue does not provide them

THREE WEEKS BEFORE

- Choose fashion show music and develop the choreography
- Plan decorations
- Finalize all flowers and accessories for each gown
- Hold a fashion show rehearsal
- Begin to develop a sheet detailing information to each vendor
- Send a second mailing to those on your list who have not yet replied
- Contact the media regarding a possible news story

TWO WEEKS BEFORE

- Develop a schedule of events and distribute to each vendor
- Develop a backstage schedule for the fashion show. Distribute copies to all backstage workers, and have several extra to post
- Consult with the fashion show vendors as to how they wish to identify their gowns
- Begin a fashion show lineup

- Have another fashion show rehearsal
- Print vendor name tags
- Print door prize tickets
- Provide a room layout to those who are setting up
- Complete the programs and have them printed
- Complete the fashion show narration and begin to practice
- Complete a list of items you need for the fashion show
- Follow up with the media

ONE WEEK BEFORE

- Start to collect items for the fashion show
- Start to collect items to take with you to the show. Use your emergency bag for ideas
- Sort vendors' name tags by booth
- Hold a dress rehearsal for the fashion show
- Make hair appointments for yourself and the models

THE NIGHT BEFORE

- Be on hand during the set-up to answer questions and solve any problems that arise
- Get a good night's sleep

BEFORE THE SHOW OPENS

- Tour the finished booths
- Put the finishing touches on your own booth

AFTER THE SHOW

- Thank each vendor by card or letter
- Thank each door prize donor. Provide the names and address of the winner(s)
- Provide the vendors with a contact list of the address and telephone numbers of the brides who attended the show

- Sit down and detail the good and the bad. This will be valuable when you plan your next show

Fashion Show Checklist

LOCATION ARRANGEMENTS
Date
Location
Time
Show begins
Rehearsal 1
Rehearsal 2
Dress rehearsal
Other notes

ROOM ARRANGEMENTS
Seating capacity
Runway
Microphone
Podium
Lighting
Music
Dressing room (female models)
Dressing room (male models)
Other notes

FEMALE MODELS (circle Bride/Maid of Honor/Bridesmaid/Mother)
B MH BM M Name and telephone number
B MH BM M Name and telephone number
B MH BM M Name and telephone number
B MH BM M Name and telephone number
B MH BM M Name and telephone number

MALE MODELS (Circle Groom/Best Man/Usher/Father)
G BM U F Name and telephone number
G BM U F Name and telephone number
G BM U F Name and telephone number
G BM U F Name and telephone number
G BM U F Name and telephone number

CHILD MODELS (Circle Flower Girl or Ring Bearer)
  FG RB Name and telephone number
  FG RB Name and telephone number

DRESSERS

1. Name and telephone

    Assigned models:

    Responsible for gown numbers:

2. Name and telephone

    Assigned models:

    Responsible for gown numbers:

3. Name and telephone

    Assigned models:

    Responsible for gown numbers:

4. Name and telephone

    Assigned models:

    Responsible for gown numbers:

5. Name and telephone

    Assigned models:

    Responsible for gown numbers:

BACKSTAGE MANAGER
  Name and telephone number
  Notes

FASHION SHOW COORDINATOR
  Name and telephone number
  Notes

COMMENTATOR
  Name and telephone number
  Notes

MUSIC
Name and telephone number
Notes

LIGHTING
Name and telephone number
Notes

DECORATOR
Name and telephone number
Notes

FLORIST
Name and telephone number
Notes

PERSON RESPONSIBLE FOR GOWN FITTINGS
Name and telephone number
Notes

PERSON RESPONSIBLE FOR TUXEDO FITTINGS
Name and telephone number
Notes

VENDORS
Bridal gowns
Bridesmaids and flower girls
Mothers
Men's wear
Accessories
Notes

FITTINGS

1. Place

    Date
    Time

2. Place

    Date
    Time

3. Place

    Date
    Time

PROGRAMS
Printer
Order deadline
Pick-up date

For Your Notes

10

FINANCIAL MANAGEMENT

Raising Your Fees (or Lowering Them)

Right now you're thinking, "Did I read that correctly? *Lower* my fees?" There are actually times when lowering your fees might seem like a good move. If you haven't been attracting enough business, it may be because your fees are too high. The best way to lower your fees is to offer a limited-time special. That way, you can raise them again if you wish.

Fees are more often raised than lowered. There are several ways to tell if the time is right for an increase.

Raise your fees if the competition raises theirs. If your fees are lower than those of other wedding planners in town, people might wonder why.

If a client seems surprised how reasonable your fees are, you should seriously consider charging more.

If you already have all the work you can handle, this would be a good time to make the increase. Having that much business is a sign that you're doing something right. A fee increase should affect new clients only, and assuming you're too busy to accept new clients at this time, this will allow you a transition period.

Some wedding planners raise their fees every year. This is certainly necessary if your expenses have increased substantially. Annual increases should not affect your current clients.

Never apologize to a client who thinks your fees are too high—lawyers and dentists never do. You are a professional, providing a valuable service. Your time and expertise are included in your fee. Never allow anyone to devalue them. By showing confidence in your fees, you are showing confidence in yourself and your abilities.

Your Accountant

Your accountant will become your best advisor, so choose wisely. Look for an accountant who specializes in home businesses, or who is familiar with the special tax implications involved. I like to call my accountant a "weapon of mass deductions!"

Ask other home business owners for referrals. Before making a final decision, meet with the accountant and be sure this is a person with whom you can develop a rapport.

Assist your accountant by finding out which method he or she uses. Many accountants like the double-entry method of bookkeeping. Others make use of the new software programs. Keep your records up-to-date. Have all receipts in order. The office-at-home expense and the depreciation of your equipment will not show up in your daily bookkeeping. Your accountant will tell you which documents to keep in order to take advantage of these deductions.

The Operating Budget

Your income, naturally, will come from the fees you charge your clients. Your expenses will be listed in two columns, estimated and actual. These are the areas in which you spend money. Expenses include but are not limited to such items as:

- loan repayment
- interest charges
- bank service charges
- office supplies
- your drawings (or salary, if you are incorporated)
- telephone
- postage
- printing and photocopying
- insurance
- advertising
- legal fees

- accountant's fees

- repairs and maintenance

- transportation

- depreciation

- office-at-home expenses

At the end of the year, the actual figures will be used to prepare your profit and loss statement. Clearly, if your income is less than your expenses, you will have a loss for the fiscal year.

Accepting Credit Cards

Some wedding planners accept credit cards for their planning services and for merchandise they sell through their businesses. Others have decided it's unnecessary. Unlike retail businesses, wedding planners do not generate impulse sales for which credit cards are often used. Clients meet with you on an appointment basis. If they do not give you a deposit in person, they'll mail a check with their signed contract. Before the wedding, they will give you a check to cover the balance. If a bride asks if you accept credit cards, tell her that you find the fees too high to justify passing them on to your clients.

Every sale is subject to a discount rate. This is the fee you pay the credit card company, in addition to a transaction fee. There is a monthly rental charge on the processing equipment or software, usually on a two-year lease. You are committed to this, regardless of how much business you actually process on the cards. There is also an application fee, which is payable even if you are declined.

If you decide to become a card merchant, make an appointment with your bank manager to start the application process. Once you are approved, you will be shown how to process your sales. As a credit card merchant, you will be able to display the logo of the card on your advertising.

Accepting credit cards on your Web site is much easier if you sign up with one of the third party credit card companies. *Sandcastles* has been doing this for years. You will be provided with the html, which you will add to your Web pages. One click will take the client into the purchasing process, which is easy and totally secure. You will receive an e-mail informing you of the details of the transaction. The funds are charged to the client's credit card and remain in your account until you have them transferred to your own bank. There is a fee for this service, but you may find that the increase in your sales more than compensates for that.

Entertaining Clients

There will be times when you do not want to meet clients at your office or their home, perhaps because you are located far from each other and agree to meet halfway. Or, you may be spending the day showing reception venues to a client and decide to stop for lunch. These are just two situations in which you will find yourself entertaining clients. In fact, coffee and lunch are regular events.

As a professional, show good manners and pick up the check. Naturally, you won't suggest a restaurant beyond your means in order to impress your clients. Pay for coffee out of petty cash, and use your business credit card or debit card for meals. You can deduct fifty percent of your own meal as a business expense. Your accountant will explain how to handle the transaction in the books.

Home Office Deductions

Home businesses generate such an attractive income tax deduction that many small business owners move back into the home after a short time in rented office space! Most of the expenses that a homeowner encounters are eligible, including the following:

- rent payment or mortgage interest
- insurance
- telephone
- property taxes
- maintenance
- heating
- water
- electricity
- repairs

The deduction is calculated according to the space your business occupies. If you have an eight-room home, your home office will account for one-eighth. On the other hand, you may be lucky enough to have an entire floor at your disposal. If your business takes up one floor in a three-floor home, you can deduct one-third.

Your accountant will guide you through the process of claiming this deduction. Save all receipts, invoices, and assessments in a separate envelope marked "Office at Home Expenses." They will not form part of your daily business transactions, and therefore they do not appear in your bookkeeping.

There are a few rules, which your accountant will explain to you. For example, the space must be used exclusively for business, so a dining room table that doubles as a part-time desk doesn't qualify. A home office expense cannot be used to create a loss for the year, but any unused portion can be carried forward into following years.

Bookkeeping Schedule

DAILY

- Summarize income
- Record expenditures

WEEKLY

- Track accounts receivable
- Track accounts payable

MONTHLY

- Close and balance cash book
- Reconcile bank account
- Reconcile petty cash
- Age accounts receivable (30, 60, or 90 days)

ANNUALLY

- Close and balance books
- Post to general ledger (your accountant will do this for you)
- Prepare income tax

Day-to-Day Bookkeeping

It is important that you keep up with the daily transactions of your business. You will be responsible only for the bookkeeping; your accountant will take care of the rest.

Bookkeeping can be done by computer or on paper. If you choose to use one of the many software programs on the market, simply follow the instructions. To do your bookkeeping on paper, purchase a cash book (also called a cash journal) from any office supply store. These books feature ruled pages and multiple columns. Choose the one with the number of columns you need.

With "double-entry" bookkeeping, each transaction is credited to one column (or account) while being debited from another. Your debits and credits will cancel each other out. If they don't, you have made an error. The main advantage of this system is that errors are easily detected.

The system is quite simple, although the "bank" account causes some confusion. When you deposit money into the bank, you record it as a debit. A withdrawal or a check drawn on the bank is recorded as a credit. It sounds as if it should be the other way around. Just accept that this is the way it works and it shouldn't give you too much trouble.

Set up the columns as follows:

- Date

- Bank, 1 column marked DR (money you put into the bank). 1 marked CR (money you take out of the bank)

- Income, CR

- Drawings, DR (money you draw out of the business); CR (money of your own that you put into the business, or business expenses that you pay out of your own pocket)

- Equipment, DR

- Petty Cash, DR

- Office Supplies, DR

- Bank Charges, DR

- Advertising, DR

- Postage and Stationery, DR

- Printing, DR

- Misc, DR (and a column named "Particulars")

- Any other columns you will use often, such as transportation, and telephone (if you have a phone line exclusive to the business)

When a bride pays you and you deposit the check in the bank, record the transaction under the columns "Income CR" and "Bank DR" on the same line. Since the debit and credit cancel each other out, you know that the transaction was recorded correctly.

If you use your business debit card to pay for office supplies, record the transaction as a debit to office supplies and credit to the bank.

If you draw money from the bank as part of your salary, record it as a debit to drawings and a credit to the bank.

If you pay for photocopying out of your own pocket, the transaction will be recorded as a credit to drawings and a debit to printing.

The Miscellaneous column is for items that show up every six months or less. Note the details in the Particulars column.

When you sign a contract or letter of agreement for a $1,000 job and receive a fifty percent deposit, you have created an "accounts receivable" of $500. The $1,000 total fee is a credit to income on the day the deposit is received. The $500 deposit you receive is deposited into the bank, creating a debit to the bank and the remaining $500 is a debit to accounts receivable. When the final payment is received, the check is deposited as a debit to the bank and a credit to accounts receivable.

If you buy a new computer at a cost of $2,000 and pay a $500 deposit, you have created an "Accounts Payable" of $1500. Record the total cost of $2000 as a debit to equipment, the $500 deposit as a credit to the bank, and the $1,500 balance as a credit to accounts payable. Each payment is a credit to the bank and debit to accounts payable.

At the end of the month, draw a red line underneath the last entry. Add up all the columns, using pencil until you are sure your calculations are correct. All of the debit columns and all of the credit columns must add up to the same number and theoretically you will end up with zero when you subtract one from the other.

Petty Cash

There will be times when you want to do a couple of dollars' worth of photo-copying or buy a few stamps. For these small purchases, your business will need a petty cash account.

At the bank, cash a check that you have made out to "cash." Fifty dollars is a good amount. When you enter this into your cash book, it will be a credit to the bank and a debit to petty cash. Keep this money in an envelope. Whenever you make a cash purchase from the petty cash envelope, put the receipt in the envelope. At all times, your receipts plus your cash will equal exactly fifty dollars.

Eventually, the cash in your envelope will get down to around three dollars. At this point, you will need to replenish the petty cash. Add up all receipts and make a check out to "cash" for this amount. Cash the check and put the money in the envelope, restoring the petty cash to fifty dollars.

In the meantime, record this transaction in the cash book as a credit to the bank and a debit to each of the applicable columns for which you have receipts.

Profit and Loss Statement

Based on the daily records that you provide, your accountant will prepare your profit and loss statement, which you will file with your tax return. This document is an overall view of your business activities for the year, and neatly summarizes the amounts spent in each of the major categories.

Most importantly, it allows you to see at a glance how much profit (or loss) your business made in the last year. Therefore, it is a useful tool in the development of your future goals.

Most small businesses operate at a loss for the first two years, sometimes longer. Accountants work hard to find tax loopholes for their clients, and a business loss is one of those.

NSF Checks

If the bank should return a bride's check after the wedding, chances are you will get a replacement and an apology. Simply place a friendly telephone call to the couple when they return from their honeymoon. The clients must also reimburse you for the NSF fee that the bank charged to your account.

Occasionally, though, you may have to send a "notice of payment due" letter. It is generally recommend that you send three, each worded a little more strictly than the previous ones.

The first will be sent by regular mail. Simply state that the bank has informed you there are insufficient funds to cover the check. Remind the client that you have recently called and ask that payment be submitted within seven days. Provide a dollar figure.

If this doesn't work, send a second letter by registered mail with return signature. Remind the client that you have previously contacted them and that the account is now thirty days past due. Again, ask for remittance.

If a third letter is necessary, send it by registered mail with return signature. Remind the client that the account is sixty days past due and if payment has not been made within five days, you will turn the matter over to a collection agency.

Keep copies of all correspondence, including post office receipts. Examine the situation; sometimes the amount is not worth the legal fees involved to recover it. In this case, you may decide to write it off as a bad debt. Your accountant can help you do this.

Travel Expenses

Your accountant can tell you how best to claim the appropriate portion of your car expenses as a business deduction. Record-keeping will be much easier if you charge everything pertaining to the car (lease or purchase payments, insurance, gas, repairs, license renewal, etc.) on a credit card reserved just for the purpose and paid in full every month. At the end of the year, determine which percentage was business, and end up with one figure for your transportation expenses for the year.

To make it easier to figure out a ratio of business to personal use, and to support your claims if you are ever audited, keep a mileage log. Use a notebook in which you record the date, beginning mileage, ending mileage, and total miles.

If you will be planning a wedding some distance from where you live, you will most likely charge an extra traveling fee. That will reimburse you for the extra gas and the likelihood that you will need to stay in a hotel. The hotel room can be written off, so be sure to draw it to the attention of your accountant. The same applies to airfare, if you should ever have to travel on business.

For Your Notes

11

YOUR SUPPORT TEAM

Working with Vendors

Vendors provide the services or products used in the planning of a wedding. They include

- florist
- caterer
- reception venue
- photographer
- videographer
- disc jockey
- musicians
- baker
- rentals
- transportation

As a wedding planner, you will be called upon to help the bride and groom locate the vendors who will best suit their needs. You are expected to be fair, ethical, and unbiased. It is often thought that wedding planners are paid by the vendors in return for the business they bring to them. Luckily, this happens only occasionally. This is unfair to the client, because a wedding planner will be tempted to steer the client toward the vendor from whom the largest commission comes. If you have created an alliance with the vendor by accepting a commission, you may be held responsible if the contract is not honored.

In the past, wedding planners were known to add a percentage to the vendor's fee and charge this to the clients in addition to their own fee. To avoid suspicion, insist that the client work directly with the vendor. Discounts are then passed on to the client, which is how it should be.

There are a couple of advantages to having the contract in your name. You will be able to make changes without having the client do it, and it is convenient for the client to make one payment to you, rather than to the various vendors. However, the disadvantages far outweigh the advantages. Of course, the biggest disadvantage is that you are responsible if the client defaults on the payment.

Reception Venues

Wedding receptions can be held in country clubs, banquet halls, hotels, restaurants, and historical buildings, just to name a few. By recommending one from your database, you can save the bride and groom a great deal of legwork. Be sure to include a wide variety to serve every client's needs.

Many reception venues are also perfect locations for wedding ceremonies. Some even have chapels. Collect brochures to show your clients. Have floor plans ready, complete with room capacities. Take them to visit their top three choices. Until the couple has decided on the venue, you cannot plan the other details.

In the Appendix you will find an outline with which you will prepare your venue database. Begin outside; such things as parking and wheelchair access are important considerations. So are the grounds, as many couples like to have wedding pictures taken in the surrounding gardens.

Indoors, take note of the electrical outlets in the rooms, the existing décor, and the PA system. Find out what items are included, and what you must rent. This includes tables and chairs, tableware, and linens.

Is the venue licensed to sell liquor, or must your clients get their own permit? Be aware that if you get the permit in your name, you will be legally responsible if a wedding guest drinks too much, injuring himself or someone else. Find out about bartenders' fees, and the number of wait staff available for dinner.

Caterers

Many venues have an in-house or on-premise caterer. If not, you will have to locate the venue first, then the caterer. Many venues have lists of recommended caterers. In some cases you will be obliged to use one from this list. Even if you are permitted to bring in your own caterer, I recommend using one of these companies, since they are already familiar with the facilities. The exception, of course, is a wedding at which you are featuring ethnic or specialized dishes.

The caterer may or may not provide linens and china. This is one of the first things you must ask about, as renting is an extra cost to your clients. Find out what happens to the dirty dishes. Usually they will be taken away dirty and washed at their headquarters. The caterer will be happy to provide you with menus for your files, and most will allow clients to sample the food.

When helping your clients weigh the different options for their catering needs, counsel them on the ways in which costs can be unintentionally inflated. For example, buffet service uses less labor, but more food is needed, as many guests go back for seconds.

Meet with the caterer after the clients have signed the contract to discuss the wait-staff ratio, food allergies or restrictions, and the final head count.

Bakers

The wedding cake is the centerpiece of the reception. Set on its own table and cut as part of the festivities, its selection deserves special care. Bakers will allow clients to taste the cake flavors, fillings and icings. Many couples find the choices so irresistible that they order each layer in a different flavor. Be sure to choose a baker who will allow this.

Wedding cake decorators are justifiably proud of their creations. However, they won't mind if you order the cake with less icing decoration so that the florist can place real flowers on it after it has been delivered.

The cake layers can be separated by pillars, or each layer can sit on the one below it. The topper will be a keepsake for years to come. Many elaborate cakes can be designed to incorporate fountains, which are rented from the baker. If the wedding cake is very large, it can be surrounded by similarly-decorated "satellite" cakes. Bakers will also rent Styrofoam wedding cakes, which the bride and groom will pretend to cut for photographs, while a slab cake is in the kitchen being cut by the catering staff.

When the cake is delivered, be on hand to inspect it according to order specifications, and have any necessary icing touchups done. Be sure the cake is placed on its table, so that there will be no need to move it. The baker will often supply a silver cake knife; if not, have one that you can lend your clients. Be sure to return all pillars and trays to the baker after the wedding.

The "Groom's Cake" is traditionally a fruitcake, wrapped or boxed. The packaging itself is labor-intensive, so a baker is not hired to do this. Many people don't like fruitcake, and couples often decide not to include it.

Photographers

When the newlyweds return from their honeymoon, they will be anxious to see the proofs of their wedding pictures. To ensure that this is a positive experience for them, hire only the best photographers.

The couple will want to look through the photographer's portfolio, and make sure that they can develop a good rapport. If they find that their personalities clash with the photographer, their smiles will be forced, and it will show in the photographs.

Find a photographer who is skilled in a wide variety of effects. Some use a combination of color/black and white photography, and many also use sepia (brown) tones. Some couples want posed wedding pictures, while others like the photojournalistic approach; hire a photographer who can do both.

In your database, include every detail of the photo packages. There is often a substantial discount, but if the package includes items your clients don't need, it's not a good deal after all. Another point: do the bride and groom own the proofs? Most photographers will provide CDs to the couple shortly after the wedding, from which they can order their prints.

Many photographers will give the envelopes for the thank-you cards to the bride and groom before the wedding. That way, they can get a head start by addressing the envelopes.

Be sure the photographer uses a back-up camera, and speaking of back-ups, be sure he or she has another photographer to shoot the wedding in case of an emergency. I was once hired to coordinate a wedding day. The bride and groom had hired a photographer who did not have a back-up. Two days before the wedding, the groom called me in a panic. There had been a death in the photographer's family and he was unable to make the wedding. All the photographers I knew were working that day, so I did something I thought I would *never* do—I hired a photographer sight unseen straight out of the Yellow Pages! There is a happy ending to this story: he was excellent, and I used him for many weddings since.

Some photographers offer a guarantee: "If your wedding pictures are unsatisfactory, we'll retake them." This is one of the most ridiculous (if not *impossible*) things that a couple should have to go through! You will find, though, that the photographer who is willing to make this promise is the one who will never have to honor it.

Videographers

Depending upon which photographer your clients choose, it may be possible to have a videographer from the same company shoot the wedding. Perhaps they offer a package deal. Have both in your database.

Either way, there are many options when working with a videographer. Some will shoot the entire day, and then edit it to an hour-and-a-half to two hours. Others are equipped with cameras that edit on the spot.

I always recommend that my clients watch a video that he has shot. As with photography, each videographer's personality comes through in his work. His style has to match that of the bride and groom in order for them to be able to work together. He must also have a back-up person available.

Usually, the wedding video will have music, titles, and special effects. Often, childhood pictures of the bride and groom will be incorporated. Wedding guests can be interviewed, giving them a chance to send their best wishes to the newly-weds. Have your clients discuss these things with the videographer, and have him show them examples.

Editing produces a smoothly-flowing and professional documentary of the day. Advise your clients to ask for an unedited copy as well. The little mistakes and bloopers that are edited out are very funny, and will give the couple much enjoyment!

Disc Jockeys

Not all disc jockeys are created equal. Fees vary widely, as do the services that the DJ will perform. A good DJ has the talent to get the guests up and dancing, and keep them there.

Many DJs work independently, while others work for companies that book the services of each DJ on a rotating basis. Include both in your database. Often the independent DJs are less expensive, as they don't have the same overhead as the DJ companies.

On the other hand, they may lack a back-up system in case of illness. With the DJ company you never have to worry about this, as a new DJ will simply be substituted. The DJs hired through these companies are generally more mature, and are required to be suitably attired. They are not permitted to drink or smoke at the wedding. With independents, you have to make all of these points clear.

Have your clients meet with the DJ before the wedding, to go over their choices of music for the special dances, and perhaps ask for his recommendations.

They can give him an idea of the age mix of the guests, so that he can plan accordingly. They can also tell him the names of any songs they want to have played, so that he can intersperse them with requests. He knows from experience which songs are popular with groups, and he will include those as well. Have the couple provide him with a "Do Not Play" list. Songs that invoke unpleasant memories have no place at a wedding reception. The DJ will be well-aware of the legal ramifications of performing music in public. In Ontario, where I work, the S.O.C.A.N. tariff applies to public performance, even for wedding receptions.

The DJ will usually be willing to act as Master of Ceremonies, announcing the wedding party, speeches, cake cutting, and bouquet and garter throw.

Live Musicians

When we speak of musicians, we mean so many things: a string quartet, a wind trio, or a single piano for the ceremony and dinner music, and a full band for the reception. Have a wide variety in your database.

Ask if you can hear them play in person. If this is not possible, they will be happy to provide you with a demo CD. Either way, make sure that the individuals you hear are the ones who will be playing.

Find out if they belong to a union. If so, certain regulations will apply to your clients. Public performances are subject to royalty payments. Have this carefully explained in writing. Check such details as mileage charges, attire, breaks (number and length), and set-up times.

If your clients wish, one of the members (usually the leader) will act as Master of Ceremonies.

The best recommendations come from the reception venues themselves. They refer musicians who have played at their location often, so you are sure to get someone who is familiar with the acoustics of the banquet rooms.

Transportation

You must be able to locate transportation for any style wedding, and coordinate the schedules.

The most popular form of wedding transportation is the chauffeur-driven limousine. And for good reason—it's elegant, spacious, and special! It's the perfect way to get a large group of people to the church or reception together, such as six bridesmaids (and all those dresses). The limousine company will help you select the cars you need.

When interviewing limousine companies for your database, you will have an opportunity to find out how they operate. Most companies, whether they charge a flat rate or by the hour, begin and end their fee at the point of departure. Therefore, it is a good idea to have several companies in your database if your business attracts clients from a wide geographic area.

Depending on the set-up of the limousine company, it may be less expensive to rent the limousine twice: first to the ceremony and the reception, and again after the reception. Investigate and do the math.

Find out if the chauffeur carries a cell phone or pager. Get the number and give a copy to the members of the wedding party who will be driving with him. Give him your cell number as well. This will cover all bases in case of a break-down or misplaced directions.

Vintage cars are second in popularity. They can be from a particular era, such as the 40's, 50's, or 60's, or perhaps from the bride's year of birth. Maybe your clients dream of a Rolls Royce. All of these can be found in the Yellow Pages. You might also contact a local association of car buffs. Among their members you may find someone willing to rent his car. Since many of these owners are reluctant to let anyone else drive, you just may have a chauffeur included!

Many brides love the idea of a horse and buggy ride to and from the church. Find out about their policies regarding inclement weather, and be ready to recommend an alternative.

Decorators

Some reception venues need no embellishment at all. Others are a little less than perfect. For these venues, you will hire the services of a decorator. They are professionals who specialize in wedding decorating.

Decorators are able to hang tulle from the ceiling of a tent in beautiful draping swags that hide the structure. In addition they deal with lighting and accessories.

As an added advantage, they supply the materials with which they work, lowering your rental costs on such items as chair covers. These experts will thoroughly coordinate everything from the centerpieces to the special effects, keeping the color scheme in mind.

Have several in your data base, as they tend to book far in advance.

Rentals

It is not likely that you will find a rental company that provides everything you will ever need when planning a wedding, so have several in your database. Just a few of the items you will need are

- tents
- tables and chairs
- chair covers
- linen
- cutlery, china, and glassware
- silver serving pieces
- punch bowls
- arches
- wishing wells
- candle stands
- fountains
- potted trees
- portable bar
- portable washrooms
- dance floors
- gazebos

If you are planning a home wedding, you will rely heavily on rentals. Interview the couple about their needs. Calculate the number of guests before you contact the rental company, so that you will be able to get an accurate estimate.

Tents

If you are planning a garden wedding, a tent will solve all of your space problems. Your tent rental company will advise you on the size and style, as well as the many available options, including lighting, fans, heating and air conditioning, and dance floors. Be sure to record these details in your database.

Tents are available in a variety of colors, although white is the most elegant and the most popular. Palladian windows and French doors add to the ambiance.

Tents can be erected on just about any surface, but you must be sure the area is free from sprinklers, underground power lines, or cables. Grassy areas are best but *never* on freshly cut grass. Choose your flooring accordingly. Many clients cut costs by renting a dance floor and leaving the rest in grass.

A second kitchen tent is often used to give the caterers a place to work. Some companies will have an employee stay on-site in case there is a problem. Have this written into your client's contract, as well as return details.

Working with Clergy

An old friend of mine (meaning how long I've known him, not his age) is a United Church minister who has been performing weddings for forty years. His chief complaint is wedding planners who won't let him do his job, or even worse, try to tell him how to do his job!

Many priests, rabbis and ministers feel the same way. It is very important to remember that we are on his territory. We are concerned with the frivolous; he has more important concerns. A man and woman are about to take the vows that will join them for life in marriage.

The first time you meet with a member of the clergy, make it clear from the beginning that you are there to assist. It is a good idea to meet with several ministers, priests, and rabbis before you are actually hired to plan a wedding at their church or synagogue. Add them to your database. That way, you will be able to visualize during your initial consultations with the couple.

Learn the policies of each church. They include such things as

- the throwing of rice, birdseed, or confetti
- the use of flowers
- the use of thumbtacks or nails on the woodwork
- picture-taking during the ceremony
- the use of secular music

In your database, be sure to include officiants who will perform civil and non-denominational weddings at the location of your clients' choosing.

The final word when working with the clergy is this—we need them, they don't need us.

Child Care Providers

Children and weddings don't always mix, yet feelings of resentment result when the bride and groom decide to exclude them. The alternative is to provide child care services at the ceremony and reception sites.

That is what I decided to do when I first set up my business. In fact, for several weddings, I was hired *because* I provided the service.

It is important that the people you hire be experienced with children of all ages. This is especially true if there will be babies involved. No doubt you know such a person. If not, your local college may be able to recommend one of their Early Childhood Education students. Or, call a nearby daycare center. They are closed on weekends, and their staff may be willing to work for you. Even those with credentials must be screened. Hire at least two people, or three if there will be children with special needs.

The bride and groom often pay the caregivers as a service to their guests, or you can arrange to have them paid directly by the parents. I find it works well to charge per child, per hour, for every child attending, whether they will be using the service or not. That way, the caregivers are compensated for being available, and the parents can bring their children in and out as they see fit.

Investigate the church and reception venue to find the best room for the children. It should be close enough to the action that the children do not feel anxious, yet far enough away that they can nap.

Ask that the caregivers be provided with a meal, which they will eat with the children.

As many of my weddings took place in historical buildings, I did not allow crafts. Glue, paint, and crayons do not mix well with period interiors. Instead, have your caregivers provide storybooks and toys, as well as a TV, DVD, and plenty of Disney videos. Many children will also bring a favorite toy from home.

Hiring Assistants

You may someday have a wedding that is too large to handle alone. Perhaps there will be a need for you to be in two places at one time. You might have a sudden illness or an unexpected emergency. In any of these situations, you will need the help of an assistant.

Depending upon the size of your business, you may want a full-time, part-time, or casual assistant. She will be hired by you, not your clients, and will work to your specifications. You will have to advertise if you do not already have someone in mind. A simple ad in the classified section of your local newspaper will get many responses—wedding planning is a very *glamorous* job, remember? Interview the best ones and make your final choice.

Once hired, your assistant will need to be trained. No doubt, she will have had personal experience with weddings. However, you have to give her the specifics of the wedding vendors in your area, as well as anything she needs to know about the weddings you are working on.

Decide ahead of time how much you will pay, and how. Will you pay an hourly wage, a wage based on a percentage of your fee for a wedding, or a flat rate per wedding? Be prepared to give her an idea of how many weddings you will be sending her on. Above all, speak to your accountant beforehand about the complexity of paying employee wages, withholding tax, and the many forms that must be filled out.

If you will need someone on a very casual basis, you may decide not to go through all of these steps. In this case, it may be preferable for you to hire someone for an isolated day and pay her yourself.

Writing a Letter of Recommendation

If an assistant leaves you, either because of an unsatisfactory performance or because your business is too slow to keep her, you will probably be asked to give her a letter of recommendation. If she's been doing a great job, write a beautiful letter in which you praise all of her positive points.

How can you praise her positive points if you have never seen them? If she has not done a good job and you have had to let her go, remember that your priority is continuing to run your business smoothly, not preventing her from finding another job.

I always like to be positive. Instead of "Mary was lazy," you could say, "The job demanded more than Mary is physically capable of." Don't say, "Mary was rude to the clients." Say, "Mary appears to be better suited to work behind the scenes." Don't lie and say that business was slow and you had no work for her; it's illegal to lay her off for this reason and then replace her with another assistant.

Concentrate on her good points: perhaps she was always punctual, she may have been well-organized, or maybe she had a pleasant telephone personality.

Defamation and Wrongful Dismissal Lawsuits

Hopefully you will never be in the position of being sued. In the wedding-planning business, this is most likely to happen if you say something untrue about a vendor, or wrongfully dismiss an employee. Both are easily avoided.

Wrongful dismissal means just that—the employee was fired for a reason that was unfair, or for an incident in which they were not involved. Whenever you must terminate employment, always do so with verifying documents. Leave a paper trail.

Defamation is damage done to a person's reputation because of an untrue remark on your part. Defamation takes two forms. Libel refers to written statements; slander is verbal.

In order to sue for damages, the party must feel that your remarks have damaged their reputation. The statements must be proven false. No matter how embarrassing the situation, you cannot be sued for defamation of character if you have repeated a known fact. If the owner of a reception venue has been convicted of illegal business practices involving brides and grooms, you are correct to pass on this information, especially if it protects your clients. However, if you have repeated untrue gossip in order to steer the clients toward a venue of your choice, and if the party finds out, you can be sued.

If you discover that someone is spreading false rumors about you, speak to your lawyer immediately to find out your options. Remember that your good name is the most valuable thing you own, and you must protect it at all costs.

For Your Notes

12

THE PROFESSIONAL YOU

Personal Public Relations

As the heart of your business, you are creating a public relations opportunity every time you meet someone. Do you make a good impression or a poor one? Are you an asset to your business or a liability?

Always display a positive attitude toward life. Smile whenever you meet someone, but remember that it's easy to detect an insincere smile. Be friendly, never aloof or arrogant. Look to the good side of people and you will genuinely like them. Respect the opinions and rights of others.

Be a patient person. Be calm, especially when those around you are frazzled. Stand still in lineups; fidgeting makes you feel frustrated, and makes the wait seem even longer. Encourage a young cashier who seems *so* slow—it may be her first day.

Carry yourself in a way that displays your self-confidence. People will react to you differently. Know that you have value as an individual, and show that you have confidence in your professional abilities. At the same time, realize that these are a gift from God, and don't allow yourself to become too vain or proud. Feel grateful for what you have been given.

Bitterness, jealousy, and resentment are cancers that destroy you. Do some mental surgery and remove them from your life.

Always show the utmost courtesy to everyone. Never depreciate another person.

Never, *ever* become a lazy person.

Finally, never leave home without your business cards, and hand them out to everyone you meet.

Perfectionism

How many times have we all heard the expression, "Nobody's perfect," and yet we try so hard to be perfect that we fall short of our true potential. Wedding planners can easily fall into this trap. We meet brides who want their weddings to be perfect, and we try to be the perfect person to make this happen.

Break out of the rut by striving for excellence instead of perfection. Excellence *is* attainable. The funny thing is, once you try to be excellent, people will start commenting that you're perfect! Excellence means doing *your* best, not someone else's idea of best, and certainly not "good enough."

If you are able to end each day knowing that you gave your best to your friends, family, and business and that they are better because of their association with you, then you have achieved excellence.

Remember, every wedding will have some small thing go wrong, hence it is not perfect. Excellence will allow you to plan weddings so well that the little imperfections will be hardly noticeable.

Sometimes, working your hardest isn't working your best. If you are exhausted from trying and it still isn't coming together, look at *how* you're working, not *how hard*. Work smarter, not harder, and strive for excellence!

Dress for Success

For meetings, with the bride and groom or with vendors, I prefer a business suit. If the weather is very warm, a skirt and blouse or a dress is still professional. If you look good in pants, by all means wear them. Some wedding planners also wear suits to the wedding itself; I prefer something dressier.

On the morning of a wedding you may be up before the bride herself, and your day will last well into the night. It's important that you wear clothing that is comfortable, and will remain fresh-looking until the end of an eighteen-hour day. Be sure to pack an extra pair of pantyhose in case you get a run.

Color wise, avoid white. Although black has been accepted for wedding guests, many still adhere to the belief that only the bride should wear white. You don't want to offend anyone. Colors are fine, but they should not be too bright.

Use good taste at all times. Revealing clothing is always inappropriate. Your skirt must not be too short or too tight. Your heel height should be attractive with the skirt, yet comfortable enough for you to spend the day on your feet.

You are not a guest, so skip the hat.

The old adage "less is more" applies to jewelry. Be sure it doesn't clang or distract in any way. A watch is a must to keep you on schedule! I also wear a small gold name tag, so guests can identify me if they need any assistance.

Have your hair professionally done. If you color your hair, make sure the roots are touched up. Pay attention to your nails, and be sure your perfume is not overwhelming. Your makeup should be subtle.

Develop a Personal Philosophy

A personal philosophy will enrich your private and professional lives alike. Robert Louis Stevenson (1850–1894), who wrote such classics as *Treasure Island,* had such a philosophy. My mother came across it years ago shared it with me. I was so inspired that I incorporated parts of it into my life. Let me share it with you; perhaps it will become a springboard to your philosophy.

Keep busy at something. Never have time to be unhappy.

Have many interests.

Don't hold postmortems. Don't be one of those people who never get over things.

Don't borrow imaginary trouble. It is harder to deal with than the real thing.

Make up your mind to be happy. Find pleasure in the simple things.

Make the best of your circumstances. No one has everything.

Everyone has times of sorrow intermingled with gladness. Try to find the laughter through the tears.

Don't take yourself too seriously.

You can't please everyone. Don't let criticism worry you.

Don't let your neighbors set your standards. Be yourself.

Hatred poisons the soul. Don't hold grudges. Avoid people who make you unhappy.

Do what you can for those less fortunate than yourself.

Do the things you like, but stay out of debt.

Let me add one more of my own—never, *ever* compare yourself to anyone else. When you do, you look at the best of them and the worst of yourself. That's not a fair comparison. Instead use the other person as a role model.

Look After Yourself

There is no doubt about it—ours can be a grueling business at times. You will have down-days, in which you are generally relaxed and can catch up on your paperwork. These will be balanced by wedding days, when you are up early, work hard all day, and arrive home in the early hours of the next morning. Add to this the demands of family, and maybe even a full-time job. It's easy to see how it can take its toll on your health. The simple truth is this:

- You must look after yourself, so that you'll be able to look after everything else!

Start with enough sleep. This is not easy when you are working an eighteen-hour day, but most nights you can manage to get to bed early enough. The right amount of sleep is a very personal thing—take your individual needs into consideration. Sleep deprivation is the leading cause of accidents and decreased productivity. Know your limits. Take a hotel room so that you won't have to drive home after an out-of-town wedding.

Balance is the key to a healthy diet. If you are not eating right, your productivity will suffer. Supplements are good if you know you will not be getting enough of specific vitamins and minerals, but experts say they are not always necessary. The benefits of water cannot be over-emphasized. It's easy to get your eight glasses a day if you carry a bottle of spring water with you. Freeze it ahead of time and drink it as it melts, to be sure it stays cold.

Finding time to exercise is sometimes difficult if you have a busy schedule, but there are ways to fit it in. Walk instead of driving to the store. Use the stairs instead of the elevator, and place a stationary bike in front of the TV so you can ride while catching up on the news. I am lucky enough to live in a condominium with a pool, sauna and gym. Perhaps you would benefit from a membership at a twenty-four hour health club, where you can work out at your convenience.

Try to stay as stress-free as possible. That's not easy if you're a working mother, but it is essential to your health. An organized schedule and a healthy family life are the keys to mental health, according to the experts. Try meditation, yoga, or breathing techniques.

Keep your annual doctor's appointments. Prevention is still the best cure!

Shape Your Future

Always look for ways to improve yourself. Read everything you can to keep abreast of trends in the wedding industry. Extend this to the fields of fashion and interior design, which affect your daily life.

Broaden your personal horizons. Visit museums and art galleries, go to the theater, read the latest novels, and see the latest movies. Travel to a part of the world you have always wanted to visit. Learn a second (or a third) language. Get a university degree.

Add to your credentials. Take college courses or workshops in art history, interior decorating, flower arranging, wine tasting, landscape painting, or drama.

Place a great importance on the people in your life. Your husband and children, your parents, siblings, and friends, are life's greatest gifts. Enrich their lives, and allow them to enrich yours.

Become more interested and you will become more interesting. Your self-confidence will improve. Faith in your abilities is what will give you the edge you need to make your business a success.

Inspirational Quotes

Some days, everything goes wrong. At times like this, you need to be inspired. Read through these quotes—something is sure to apply to you. A few of them are credited to famous people. The others are unknown, but definitely appreciated!

We all have ability. The difference is how we use it.

Ability is what you are capable of doing. Motivation determines what you do. Attitude determines how well you do it.

It is not the client's job to remember you. It is your job to make sure they never forget you.

Life is change. Growth is optional. Choose wisely.

Success comes to those who dare to begin.

Admit you're wrong when you're wrong, and you'll be right.

All our dreams come true, if we have the courage to pursue them. (Walt Disney)

It is our attitude at the beginning of a difficult task which, more than anything else, will determine its outcome.

Discovery of a solution consists of looking at the same problem as everyone else and thinking something different.

A pessimist is one who makes difficulties of opportunities; an optimist is one who makes opportunities out of difficulties.

The best way to become a legend is to win one at a time until time makes you one of a kind.

Every path has its puddle.

Unless commitment is made, there are only promises and hopes, but no plans.

It takes five hundred small details to make a favorable impression. (Cary Grant)

Procrastination is the thief of time.

Whoever said they never had a chance, never took one.

The only way to make your dreams come true is to change them into plans.

You'll never make it to the next level by holding onto the first.

Diligence is the mother of luck. (Benjamin Franklin)

When you're through changing, you're through.

To achieve happiness in your life, you need to know only three things: what you want, what you're prepared to give up to get it, and how to keep your balance in the process.

I have failed over and over again. That's why I succeed. (Michael Jordan)

A sale will make you a living. A skill will make you a fortune.

A person who never made a mistake, never tried anything new.

I have always made a total effort, even when the odds seemed entirely against me. I never quit trying. I never felt that I didn't have a chance to win. (Arnold Palmer)

Turn contacts into contracts.

Regardless of how you feel inside, always try to look like a winner. Even if you are behind, a sustained look of control and confidence can give you the mental edge that results in victory.

We are what we repeatedly do. Excellence then, is not an act, but a habit. (Aristotle)

Some do not plant in the spring, do not work in the summer, and then expect a fall harvest.

Well done is better than well said. (Benjamin Franklin)

If something truly excites you, you will not have to be pushed. It will pull you.

Action always generates inspiration; inspiration seldom generates action. (Frank Tibot)

The best inspiration is not to outdo others, but to outdo ourselves.

Don't wait for your ship to come in. Swim out to meet it.

Keep your fears to yourself, but show your courage to others.

Obstacles are what we see when we take our eyes off our goals.

Happiness is not a goal. It's a byproduct.

Take care of the nickels and dimes, and the dollars will take care of themselves.

You are your only obstacle.

For Your Notes

Are You Ready to Take Control?

It is both frightening and comforting to realize that you are in control of your own future and that of your wedding-planning business. It's frightening because you have no one else to depend on and no one to blame if things go wrong. It's comforting because, after all, you can only depend on yourself, and the sky is the limit! The future of your business cannot be left to chance. You must carefully guide it and work hard to become the best wedding planner/CEO you can be.

The control you have is your greatest advantage.

You've heard the old saying, "You can lead a horse to water, but you can't make him drink." Remember this—it's not your job to make him drink; it's your job to make him thirsty!

In writing this book, my wish was to make aspiring wedding planners thirsty to get into this exciting and fast-growing profession. If only one of you becomes successful, I have reached my goal.

APPENDIX: VENDOR DATABASE

Developing Your Vendor Database

As your business grows, so will your list of vendors. You will discover that a certain caterer has a specialty unlike any other or that one florist is best for centerpieces. You may have used these vendors at past weddings, or maybe they were referred to you by another consultant or through networking.

To help you keep track of these vendors, I recommend the use of a vendor database. I keep mine on computer disc; you may prefer to use a three-ring binder, 3 x 5 index card system, or accordion file. File each under the appropriate category: caterers, photographers, florists, DJs, etc.

Use the following pages to begin your database. Copy them to suit your needs. Be sure to include several vendors from each category, as you will not want to operate your business without your "team" behind you!

Bridal salons have not been included in this database, as the bride and her mother usually choose the wedding gown, often before hiring the wedding planner!

Church or Ceremony Site

Name of Church

Address

Telephone

E-mail

Clergy

Are outside clergy permitted to perform the wedding ceremony?

Denomination   Seating capacity

One aisle or two?   Length of aisle

Color of carpet   Dominant color of décor

Does the church have stained glass windows?

Description of the altar

Do you have changing facilities for the bride?

Do you have reception facilities? For how many people?

Parking?   How many cars?

Additional parking?   Wheelchair entrance?

Must one be a member of the church to get married here?

Interfaith marriages? Divorced?

Is pre-martial counseling required?

How many sessions? Cost?

Candles in windows? Candleholders?

Pew bows?   Choir?

Are there any restrictions as to the time of day weddings can be preformed?

Are photography and videography allowed during the ceremony?

    Organist   Telephone

What are the restrictions on music?

Can we throw confetti? Birdseed? Potpourri?

    Fees: Church
                         Organist
                         Clergy
                         Altar boys
                         Other

Sketch of floor plan:

Officiant

Name

Telephone

E-mail

How much do you charge to perform a marriage ceremony?

How far will you travel?

Do you charge extra for travelling outside your area?

What will you wear?

How do you wish to be paid?

Reception Venue

Name

Address

Telephone

Fax

E-mail

Web site

Contact person

What is the seating capacity for a sit-down dinner?

How many rooms do you have for receptions?

    Color of carpet?   Dominant color?

In-house caterer or outside caterer?

Do you have changing facilities for the bride?

Washroom facilities?

    Parking?   How many cars?

    Wheelchair parking?   Valet parking?

    Wheelchair entrance? Elevator?

How large is the dance floor?

How many electrical outlets are in the room?

Do you provide china, glassware, cutlery, linen?

Is there a choice of colors?

Is there a PA system?

How early can we set up? When must we be out?

Can the hours be extended? What is the over-time fee?

Who is responsible for cleanup?

Do we need our own liquor license?

Can we throw confetti? Birdseed? Potpourri?

Waiters: How many? Style of dress

How much are the bartenders' fees?

How soon must we book?

What is the cost of the room rental?

How much is the deposit and when is it due?

When is the balance due?

What are your cancellation and postponement policies?

Sketch of floor plan:

Photographer

Business name

Address

Telephone

Fax

E-mail

Web site

Contact person

How long have you been in the business?

May I have some samples of your work for my business?

Will you be personally taking the pictures?

Do you have an assistant?

Do you have a back-up person in case you are unable to work the day of the wedding?

Do you carry an extra camera in case of emergency?

Do you do portraits? Engagement pictures?

Do you retouch pictures?

Do you use special effects?

How long does it take to get prints after the wedding?

How many photographs will you take in all?

How long will you stay at the ceremony?

How long will you stay at the reception?

What are your top three packages?

What size prints do you offer?

Is your travel included? If not, what is the extra cost?

What extras do you offer (albums, framing, etc)?

Will you work from a list of necessary photographs?

How far in advance do you book?

What deposit do you require, and when is it due?

When is the balance due?

What is your cancellation policy?

What is your postponement policy?

Do you guarantee a retake if the photos are unsatisfactory?

Videographer

Business name

Address

Telephone

Fax

E-mail

Web Site

Contact person

Do you specialize in weddings?

What is your price structure? Packages?

Are there any additional charges?

Do you provide duplicate discs?

Do you use special effects?

What deposit do you require?

When is the balance due?

What is your cancellation policy?

What is your postponement policy?

Do you have a back-up in case of illness?

What formats do you use?

Can my clients view a sample of your work?

What extras do you provide?

Caterer

Business Name

Address

Telephone

Fax

E-mail

Web site

Contact person

How long have you been in business?

Are you licensed to serve liquor?

What is your price structure? Are there any additional charges?

Are taxes included? Gratuities?

Is set-up included in your cost?

What deposits do you require?

When is the balance due?

What is your cancellation policy?

What is your postponement policy?

Do you provide tables, chairs, linens, china, glassware, and cutlery?

What is the charge?

Will you accommodate food restrictions? Special diets?

Will you handle arrangements for the bar and the bartender?

What is the additional charge? Is there a corkage fee?

Will you serve the punch and coffee?

Will you provide all serving help?

Will you cut and serve the wedding cake? Pack the top layer?

What is the charge?

Will you pack a light snack to go for the bride and groom?

What other extras do you provide?

Can my clients book a tasting appointment?

Florist

Business name

Address

Telephone

Fax

E-mail

Web site

Contact person

Will you build a floral scheme around color swatches?

What rental items do you provide?

Do you do floral preservations? What is the charge?

Do you deliver? Is there a charge? To which areas?

Will you set up at the ceremony and reception sites?

What deposits do you require?

When is the balance due?

What is your cancellation policy?

What is your postponement policy?

Limousine

Business name

Address

Telephone

Fax

E-mail

Web site

Contact person

What models and sizes of limousines do you offer?

What is your price per hour? Or fraction thereof?

Does that include gratuities?

Do your drivers carry cell phones or pagers?

Is there a minimum time?

What deposit do you require?

When is the balance due?

What is your cancellation policy?

What is your postponement policy?

Musicians

Business name

Address

Telephone

Fax

E-mail

Web site

Contact person

How long have you been in the business?

What kinds of music do you play?

How many members are in your band/group/ensemble?

What is your price per hour? Or fraction thereof?

Does this include gratuities?

Can my clients listen to a live demonstration or a demo CD?

Do you have references?

Is there a minimum time limit?

What about overtime?

Do you take breaks? How many?

What deposits do you require?

When is the balance due?

What is your cancellation policy?

What is your refund policy?

Do you belong to a union? What regulations apply?

When do you set up? How long does that take?

What will your members wear?

Will you act as Master of Ceremonies?

Do you supply spotlights, mirror ball, etc? What is the cost?

Do you charge for mileage? How much?

Do your members expect a meal?

Disc Jockey

Business name

Address

Telephone

Fax

E-mail

Web site

Contact person

How long have you been in the business?

What kinds of music do you play?

What is your price per hour? Or fraction thereof?

Does this include gratuities?

Do you have references?

Is there a minimum time limit? What about overtime?

Do you take breaks? How many?

What deposits do you require?

When is the balance due?

What is your cancellation policy?

What is your refund policy?

Do you belong to a union? What regulations apply?

When do you set up? How long does that take?

What will you wear?

Will you act as Master of Ceremonies?

Do you charge for mileage? How much?

Do you expect a meal?

Decorator

Business name

Address

Telephone

Fax

Web site

Contact person

What training have you had?

What services do you provide?

What items do you rent?

Can my clients see a portfolio of your work?

Can I have a price list for my files?

When do you set up and tear down?

How early must items be reserved?

What is the charge?

What deposits do you require?

When is the balance due?

What is your cancellation policy?

What is your postponement policy?

Balloonist

Business name

Address

Telephone

Fax

Web site

Contact person

What training have you had?

What types of arches do you do?

What type of centerpieces do you do?

What other services do you provide?

Do you deliver? Is there a charge? To which areas?

Will you set up at the reception site?

What is the charge?

What deposits do you require?

When is the balance due?

What is your cancellation policy?

What is your postponement policy?

Rentals

Name

Address

Telephone

Fax

E-mail

Web site

Contact person

Can I have a price list for my files?

What is your delivery and pickup policy?

How early must items be reserved?

When is the balance due?

Do you rent: Tents

Gazebos

Potted plants

Fountains

Bar

Linens

China

Cutlery

Floor candlesticks

Chair covers

Chairs

Tables

Centerpieces

Chocolate fountains

Dance floors
Arches
Portable washrooms
What else?

Do you set up and deliver?

Tents

Business Name

Address

Telephone

Fax

E-mail

Web site

Contact person

Can I have a price list for my files?

When do you set up and tear down?

How early must the tent be reserved?

When is the balance due?

Will someone stay onsite during the reception?

What sizes and types of tents do you rent?

Do you supply lighting for your tents?

What types of flooring do you offer?

Do you provide heating/air conditioning for your tents?

Baker

Business name

Address

Telephone

Fax

E-mail

Web site

Contact person

What is your most popular type of wedding cake?

What kinds of groom's cakes do you make?

What is your price structure?

May my clients taste a sample of the cake and filling?

How far in advance must the cake be ordered?

Will you deliver and set up the cake?

What deposit do you require?

When is the balance due?

What is your cancellation policy?

What is your postponement policy?

Do you furnish boxes for the cake?

When do the support pieces need to be returned?

Destination Weddings

Name of company

Address

Telephone

Fax

E-mail

Web site

Contact person

What countries or areas are covered?

What are the requirements to get a marriage license?

What is the cost?

Is there a waiting period? How long?

What documents are needed?

Do you offer wedding packages?

What is the currency in that location?

What deposit do you require?

What is your cancellation policy?

Do you supply references?

About the Author

Shari Beck is a graduate of the University of Waterloo and the New York School of Interior Design.

As the head of *Interior Motives*, Shari enjoyed a successful career in the design field, including developing and teaching an interior decorating course for a local college. She opened *Sandcastles* in 1996, to use her flair with color, fabrics and space planning in the field of wedding consulting.

Since then, Shari has helped countless brides plan their dream weddings. Her position as one of the Toronto area's foremost wedding planners has earned her the prestigious Wedding Planner Award.

As well as maintaining the award-winning *Sandcastles* Web site, Shari is a regular contributor to other wedding-planning Web sites. In her spare time, Shari has taken numerous college courses in the areas of adult education and business administration, including Business Communications, Teaching the Adult Learner, Financial Management, Marketing and Public Relations, Curriculum Development, and Business Law.

Her BA from the University of Waterloo is a unique combination of Religious Studies, Social Work, and Psychology—the perfect mix for a wedding planner. *Sandcastles* is a multifaceted wedding business, which includes wedding planning, marketing, business management, organization, and the development and administration of the popular home-study certification program for wedding planners. Shari's diverse experiences and education provide her with the perfect balance to perform all of these, and more.

Shari's other books include *Weddingology* and *The Proverbs Principle*.

978-0-595-43762-7
0-595-43762-1

Printed in Great Britain
by Amazon.co.uk, Ltd.,
Marston Gate.